Joe Barnes is a graduate of the University,
having gained an honours degree in Political Science. Since
then, he has walked a far from conventional path. First
training in tennis coaching and then hypnotherapy, he now
runs his own academy and practice. He's trained players
who have gone on to play at national level and helped
numerous clients give up smoking, lose weight, rediscover
their confidence and overcome fears. He now runs the
Screw the System website, blogs, vlogs, speaks and coaches.

ESCAPE THE SYSTEM

Break Free from the 9 to 5,
Pursue your Passion
and Live the Life you Want

JOE BARNES

Dedication:

To the memory of Kalief Browder and all the heroes
who stand up for what's right

ESCAPE THE SYSTEM

Special Offer

As a thank you for purchasing this book, I want to give you a FREE copy of my course, *How to Escape The System: The 30 Day Challenge to Break Free from the 9 to 5, Find your Passion and Overcome your Fears.*

The course builds on this book, giving you some clear actionable steps you can take over the next 30 days to lay the foundations for living the life you want. You will learn,

- How to identify a passion you can make a living from.
- A two-step strategy you need to be successful doing it.
- How to overcome the inevitable adversity you'll face.
- How to overcome your fears and realise your potential.

To claim your FREE copy, visit www.screwthesystemnow.com/escape2/ and enter your email in the sign-up box. You'll then be directed towards the instructions for downloading the course and added to the monthly newsletter.

Connect with me

I love hearing from my readers, so please get in touch. Whether you have a question, feedback or something you want to discuss, I look forward to hearing from you. Connect here,

Facebook: www.facebook.com/joebarnes1980/
YouTube: www.youtube.com/user/KnowJoe19/
alternatively, channel is called ScrewTheSystem
Twitter: @screwthesystem1
Instagram: screwthesystem19
email: joe@screwthesystemnow.com

I see all this potential and I see it squandered. An entire generation pumping gas, waiting tables, slaves in white collars. Advertising has us chasing cars and clothes, working jobs we hate so we can buy shit we don't need. We are the middle children of history. No purpose, no place. We have no great war, no great depression. Our great war is a spiritual war; our great depression is our lives. We've all been raised on television to believe that one day we'll all be millionaires and movie gods and rock stars. But we won't. We're slowly learning that fact. And we're very, very pissed off.

- Chuck Palahniuk (*Fight Club*)

Introduction

I've always been told it's important to keep your audience in mind. However, as I sat down to write this book my mind drew a blank. I tried to create an image of what they might look like, how old they'd be or where they'd work, but my attempts were in vain. No matter what I did, I just couldn't seem to define my target audience.

So, I put the thought to the back of my mind and concentrated on starting the book.

As soon as I did this, though, the answer hit me. I had a clear picture of exactly who it was for. However, rather than being the image of a total stranger, or somebody I knew who was down on their luck, the picture I saw was of myself. It was me, aged 20, at possibly the lowest point in my life.

As I looked back on myself, I saw someone very different to who I am now. This person was confused about the direction his life was heading and full of self-doubt. He'd

1

been raised on images of film and sports stars accomplishing amazing feats, heroic tales from history books and novels and somehow assumed he would follow a similar path. Now, as he entered adulthood, he could see this wasn't going to be the case. Instead, all that awaited was the reality of working endless hours in a job that provided nothing more than financial reward. Perhaps he would earn enough money to live in a nice neighbourhood and go on two holidays a year, but his prospects didn't stretch much beyond that. In fact, there was a good chance he would live without any great adventure or calling as his childhood dreams faded into insignificance.

What ate at him the most, though, was the emptiness of having nothing to believe in. Religion was see through, materialism, the quickest route to a life devoid of meaning and charity, largely ineffective in a world that undervalued its role. He had no role model to emulate and no path to pursue. As a result, he felt frustrated and trapped. Moments of depression were not uncommon and although convinced there was more to life than what was being offered, he had no idea as to what this might be.

This book is for that confused 20-year-old, yet its scope reaches much further than one individual. It's a call to arms for all entrepreneurs and people with a so-called crazy dream. If you've ever felt that you could be doing something greater with your life than you presently are, then you'll discover that you can and will. If you've recently left the education system and are totally uninspired by the prospects laid out before you, then you'll find answers and direction. If you're an outsider and feel excluded by a society that doesn't care, then you'll find a home within these pages. If you feel trapped in a career you've been working in for years, then you'll discover how to walk a new path. If you're experiencing the so-called midlife crisis and wondering where all the years have gone, then you'll find your new lease of life. If you're fed up of having to conform to somebody else's standards of working and living, then you'll discover how to live by your own. And if you're depressed, or even suicidal, then you'll find those vital ingredients – purpose and meaning – that will reconnect you with the joy of life.

There is a battle that rages throughout our lives. At some point we are all faced with the choice of whether to be true to our desires, beliefs and conscience or let our fears and the expectation of what we "should" be doing determine our decisions.

Perhaps you've felt this battle raging in you. Not content with mediocrity, you're aware there is something out there greater than the life you know. Furthermore, you know there's truer version of yourself you're *meant* to be. Between these ideals and your reality, lies every occasion you've kept quiet when you should have spoken up, taken the safe option for fear of what you might lose and let the daily grind blind you from the bigger picture.

Can you make the leap? It's a tough call when staying true to your dreams and desires appears to be a naïve step destined to end in disaster. Many don't even have the first idea about what their life's purpose might be. As a result, it's no surprise the vast majority of us accept The System and ignore our soul's desperate cries for something greater.

We don't go without a struggle though. Who, at the

outset, would tolerate years spent stuck in traffic, attending pointless meetings, working a stressful job and consuming in ever greater quantities to make themselves feel better? It all seems such a terrible waste, yet when you're living in what you believe to be the reality of 21st century life, it somehow appears unavoidable.

But what if there was another way? What if you could live a life where you didn't have to compromise yourself to be successful? What if you could live and work with people and ideas that truly inspired you? Would it be worth taking the risk and looking beyond what you've been led to believe is the way the world works?

The System's Solution

The System has its own way of dealing with people who spend too long dwelling on the battle between desire and expectation. We're encouraged to manage our discontent and frustration by treating the *symptoms* of our problems. If you're depressed then pop another pill, if you're lonely then join a group, if you're bored then escape your reality through drugs, alcohol, music, computer games or TV. The message is clear; sweep your issues under the carpet and under no circumstance question the reasons why you feel disconnected from life.

The outcome of this approach is that the individual is led to believe there is something wrong with *them*. Without the in-depth scrutiny that might lead you to discover The System's deficiencies, it's all too easy to continue believing you must accommodate yourself to the way it works. After all, it's a huge entity that supports life for billions of people, how could one individual's feelings be relevant when compared to the legitimacy of this behemoth?

Such an understanding is convenient for The System because its legitimacy never gets questioned. It remains the keeper of the truth and the true representation of life as we know it. As a result, we find ourselves in a position where we seek to please The System. Our beliefs and desires have to change to match what's acceptable. Furthermore, our decisions and actions must be altered after careful consideration of the impact they might have on our standing.

After all this suppression, is it any wonder that we experience a spiritual fall out? With suicide in the UK among 18 – 34-year-old males claiming more lives than AIDS, road accidents and murder combined[1] and prescription drug use in the US rising to 48% of the population over the age of 12[2], it appears we are the lost generation. A life without purpose has led us to desperate measures in our attempts to escape.

If treating the symptoms of our discontent fails, then The System has another alternative - *denial*. When we all follow the crowd and turn a blind eye to our frustrations, there's nobody left to expose our true feelings. We may hate our jobs and, in some cases, our lives, but when someone asks us how we're doing, we reply, "fine." Although a seemingly insignificant response, its evidence of an attitude that wants to mask what we really feel. Keeping up with the next person is a system obsession and nobody wants to appear the odd one out. As a result, we create a reality where everybody's doing fine and we simply don't talk about the things we're not happy with.

The outcome of this denial is a belief there is little to be done about the defects of modern life. We may not like it, but it's normal to work 50- or 60-hour weeks and get little time to spend with our loved ones. We may despise the fact that we can't attach any greater meaning to our life than making money to survive, but complaining about it only makes us stand out in a system where most people seek to hide. As a result, subconsciously, we feel helpless and trapped. Although we may never publicly express it, we resign ourselves to life being incomplete.

These are The System's two ways of assisting anyone who feels dissatisfied or confused with life – gloss over or deny it. Needless to say, I found both approaches difficult to stomach. The thought of having to live my life pretending that everything was ok, or denying my true desires, was too stifling to accept. Instead, I had to find answers. I had to see if I could push the boundaries and discover a life outside The System. . .

The Answer

Fortunately, after many years of struggle, I found my answer. This answer freed me from the fear of challenging The System's expectations and enlightened me to the possibility of living life on my terms. However, in trying to communicate it to a wider audience, I come up against a serious obstacle.

The System conditions us to put limits on our ambitions and modify our desires. *Be realistic*: It's a mantra designed to protect us from the massive disappointment of discovering that both ourselves, and the world we live in, are full of limitation. By following it, we'll never have our hearts broken, dreams shattered or self-esteem crushed.

Contrary to this conditioning, my answer told me I had to leave myself completely *open*. In the pursuit of a life outside the constraints of The System, I had to be prepared to experience every kind of emotion; the dejection of continual failure, the delight of eventual success and everything in between. In short, I had to become *alive* to life. I had to take a leap into the unknown and believe that, somehow, I would fly.

The System warns against this. Above all else, it tells us not to give in to our dreams. It informs us that we are very ordinary and should be happy for what we've got. As a result, you may find yourself having to free your mind from a lifetime of conditioning. You have to get your head round the idea that *allowing yourself to believe in the seemingly impossible will give you strength*, rather than set you up for disaster.

Of course, The System will seek to dissuade you at every opportunity. Until you learn to silence its voice, there will be constant reminders about the dangers of the path you've chosen. It will tempt you with its reward of security and comfort and, for a lot of people, the thought of losing these will be enough to scare them back into the fold.

For you, however, this is no longer an option. The System's model of accepting commands and emulating behaviour and outlook is gone. It may have served a purpose in finding you a place in the world, but it will only take you so far. If you want more than a copy of somebody else's life, then you'll have to learn how to lead your own.

This is something The System doesn't teach. You'll only

find this kind of knowledge from sources that don't claim to know the truth. **This book is one of them.**

It gives you permission to be pissed off with life and frees you from the need to put on a show. Furthermore, it supports you in your right to expect more than working a 9 – 5 for 40+ years of your life and an existence focused on mortgages, pensions and an early retirement. It asks you to set your sights higher than living for the weekend and those precious few weeks' holiday a year. By applying its insights you'll be shown how to walk a greater path and eventually forge an existence untouched by the limitations of The System.

A Search for Meaning

A deeper understanding of life is usually gained when a person faces some kind of life challenge or struggle. This was certainly the case with me. Although I had a happy childhood, by the time I reached adolescence, cracks started to appear.

These cracks deepened and reached a critical point at university. It was here my life began to fall apart. I'll now share with you my story and explain how I became switched on to the idea of escaping The System.

It all started while I was at university, studying for a degree in political science. Many might say their university days are the best of their lives but for me it was the opposite. In fact, my life had been in a free fall ever since I enrolled. While my peers were out partying, I was experiencing a mid-life crisis at the age of 20.

This crisis began within two months of arriving at

university. Even at this early stage, I'd had enough of academic study. I was hungry to live and experience all life had to offer. Instead, I found myself stuck in a library scouring through books on political theory and government systems. It wasn't for me. I had no real passion or interest in what I was learning.

My disillusionment with the course made me think deeply about my life beyond university. I began to realise that without a passion or interest to follow, I'd always be chasing a carrot that I'd never get to enjoy. A degree wasn't an end point, it was only the beginning. Then I had to find a job. Once I had a job, I had to gain promotion. Then I had to climb many rungs up the ladder until maybe 20 years down the line I might be in a senior position. Even then, I couldn't enjoy the moment because I would be working towards my retirement, putting enough money aside so that I could wait for my death in comfort.

For a 20-year-old, hoping for some great adventure, it seemed like a bleak picture. The thing that got me the most was the thought I'd always be *working towards something*, never enjoying the moment. Of course, if I liked my work then this would be fine, but what if a future career provided as little stimulation as my degree?

These thoughts ate away at me throughout my time at university. As a result, I became demotivated and lost all belief in what I was doing. My degree, rather than being an enjoyable learning experience, became nothing more than a certificate on a piece of paper.

My crisis deepened as I found it increasingly difficult to integrate with my fellow students. At the time, I didn't drink and with alcohol being such a fundamental part of the social scene, I found it virtually impossible to make friends. Partying, clubbing and socialising, for many, seemed to be the highlight of the university experience. For me, it was something I just couldn't relate to. All I saw was a group of 18 – 22-year olds conforming to expectations of how they *should* have fun. It was as if we were *under pressure* to go out, get drunk and party. We were students, it was expected of us.

However, I failed to see the value of drinking myself to the point where I couldn't remember what I'd done the night before, or felt ill the next day. It may have provided a sense of release, but night after night of "big nights out" just distracted from the bigger picture of where my life was heading.

With such an outlook, it was clear I would struggle to fit in. It was no surprise that, as the weeks passed, I found myself slipping further and further into my own insular world. Apart from the exchange of pleasantries with course mates and meetings with tutors, human contact was rare. Without a group of friends or girlfriend, I had no one to confide in or share good times with. All I had was my room, my thoughts and a seemingly endless amount of time to dwell on my miserable situation.

Possibly as a result of my self-imposed confinement, I developed a bizarre string of psychosomatic illnesses. Insomnia, irritable bowel syndrome, chronic shoulder pain and an unexplainable bloodshot eye, drained me of energy and also had a profound impact on my state of mind. From being a keen sportsman who trusted his body, I was beginning to feel weak and vulnerable. I spent the days fretting about getting enough sleep; concerned about how bloated I felt, self-conscious if somebody looked me in the eye and worried my shoulder would never heal.

In an attempt to find a remedy for my ailments, I went to see different doctors but they all informed me there was nothing medically wrong. This confused me as discomfort and a lack of energy was something I lived with on a daily basis. However, without the assistance of a doctor, there didn't seem like much I could do.

As I moved into my third and final year, I'd endured two meaningless years studying a course I didn't like, worrying about medical conditions that didn't exist and spending most of my time alone. The prospect of completing university should have felt like a relief. However, as I looked to the future, there was an even greater threat lurking on the horizon.

Decision Time

Ironically, by the end of my time at university, I began to find some common ground with my fellow students. After having spent three years choosing when we attended lectures and only working if an essay was due, we now faced a massive upheaval. Free time was about to become a thing of the past. Upon entering the world of work, we would be required to slave away for almost the entire year as past times and passions had to be sacrificed at the altar of our all-important careers.

I was not alone in feeling slightly apprehensive about the prospect of giving 50 hours a week to a job I didn't believe in. The general mood was one of unease. We may be relatively well paid in our graduate careers but if we never had any time to appreciate life, then what was the purpose of all that money?

As restrictive as the working hours appeared, though, this wasn't the main concern. What worried us the most was the unappealing nature of the work we were required to undertake. Time and again, I heard students talking in canteens and libraries about their lack of interest in potential careers. It seemed that traditional graduate jobs offered very little in terms of personal reward.

Few wanted to spend their lives working on accounts, thumbing through endless laws, advising people on insurance or telling someone where to invest their money. However, rather than looking at other avenues, it seemed the antidote to this problem lay in convincing yourself it was only a stop gap measure. After a few years, we'd magically find something that sparked our interest and everything would be alright.

Having spoken with people in their 30s and 40s, though, I knew this wasn't the case. The most common explanation I heard from this generation was that they had "drifted" into their line of work, committing to it with the intention of finding a more fulfilling role a down the line. Of course, this rarely happened. By that stage, they had a family to support, and what they believed to be the financial necessities of modern life, prevented them from ever pursuing their dreams.

As I listened to the stories of older generations and the concerns of my peers, I started to wonder if they were using The System as an excuse. As hard as it is to commit to a career that brings little sense of fulfilment, was it not a whole lot harder to strike out on your own?

With the pressure of meeting expectations and so many reasons to conform, maybe it was just easier to slide into mediocrity. At least, when doing so, you could claim everybody else was making the same decision and therefore, it was justified. After all, if we were all being sold down the river, none of us would be rude enough to point out how fast the current was moving, taking us further and further away from any dreams we once had.

All these thoughts were taking on a very real significance because I could see I was faced with a dilemma. They became even more poignant when I stumbled upon a new interest that took me in an unexpected direction.

A New Direction

While in my final year at university, I visited a hypnotherapist to treat my insomnia. To my surprise, the treatment was very effective and after only a few sessions my sleeping greatly improved. This transformation left me curious to find out more. As I began to research the subject, I had the idea of studying a course with a view to practicing hypnotherapy. For the first time in 3 years, my life felt like it had a meaning.

Finding this outlet was not all positive though. When I explained my post-university plans to my parents and careers advisors, they both rubbished the idea of becoming a hypnotherapist. They asked me to consider how I was going to support myself, what other people might think and whether it might lead to isolation from my peer group. I wasn't prepared for this barrage of negativity and in my weakened state, began to believe their opinions.

This left me in a dilemma. On the one hand, I didn't want to spend my life feeling like I had to meet other people's expectations. On the other, if I broke free from The System's path, all I could see was years of hardship and struggle. I was torn. My rational mind told me pursuing hypnotherapy as a 22-year-old politics graduate was completely unheard of. However, my gut told me something exciting was about to occur.

I toiled with both arguments for days on end until finally, unable to decide, I prayed for help. Not a religious person, this act seemed quite odd. In my state of desperation, though, it felt like the only option available.

Whether merely a coincidence or a genuine case of divine intervention, the very next day my prayers were answered. While searching through my bookcase I came across a book I'd bought the previous year. At the time, I'd read it, found it interesting and then discarded it when preparation for my exams got underway. Now, as I flicked through the contents, it seemed as if the answer to my dilemma was contained within its pages.

The book was *The Power of Your Subconscious Mind* by Joseph Murphy, written in 1963 and a classic in the personal-development world. Its lessons about the importance of belief, information on how to use your mind to heal ailments and sections about the significance of thoughts and feelings all came alive, seemingly written for me, at this point in my life. I was gripped from the opening passage:

> I have seen miracles happen to men and women in all walks of life all over the world. Miracles will happen to

you, too – when you begin to use the magic power of your subconscious mind. This book is designed to teach you that your habitual thinking and imagery mold, fashion and create your destiny. For as a person thinketh in his subconscious mind, so is he.[3]

This simple positive voice made the world of difference. It was the only outlet that suggested I could live the life I wanted. A meaningful, exciting and fulfilling future lay ahead if I could master this power. It was a revelation.

I raced through the rest of the book in a matter of days, and, as I absorbed its lessons, had a further insight. It came to me one evening while I was contemplating my future and was the answer I'd been looking for.

I will come to the exact nature of this new understanding in the next chapter, but suffice to say, the dilemma I'd been facing became almost inconsequential. I knew what I had to do and this revelation gave me the strength to believe I could handle any situation.

* * *

Why is this book called *Escape The System*? I chose this title because it summarises my quest. Throughout my life I have been told what I should be doing, pressured to conform and expected to sacrifice my desires so that I didn't rock the boat. This was presented to me as the route to success. However, from my position on the periphery of my peer group, I could see something else. I began to realise that, as life continued, it was the people who willingly played by the rules and conformed to every expectation that got screwed. A lifetime of endless working hours would play havoc with their health. An over reliance on other people and organisations left them stranded when situations like redundancy occurred. And a commitment to a line of work that provided little stimulation robbed them of all vitality.

The System chewed up these people. They chose their path with promises of security and wealth but only found boredom and restriction. I was fortunate to see this from an early age, but without the awareness of another path, many believe there is no other option than to conform. This book suggests otherwise. By revealing how to break free from The System, you will be given the opportunity to be truly great.

Most success manuals don't offer this opportunity. While they teach you the principles of success, what they fail to address is on whose terms that success is enjoyed. Sure, you can gain promotion, increase your income, acquire more friends, get married and have a family, but what if you end up feeling miserable? If you're trying to succeed according to The System's definition then you could be ignoring your own deeper calling.

That won't happen with this book. I am about to present you with the only path to being truly free. Because the main cause of your discontent is acknowledged and addressed – being raised in a system that encourages conformity to a stiflingly limited life while ignoring the magnificence of your individuality and dreams – the success you create for yourself will enrich you in a way that nourishes your soul.

And, should you wish to walk it, I will present you with

the only path to shaping the course of history. Because, make no mistake, the Einstein's, Columbus's, Darwin's and Mandela's of this world didn't get to where they did by following the rules. They got to where they did because they existed, and most importantly *thought*, outside the boundaries of The System. This is the only way to make the impossible become possible.

Should you need reassuring, such luminaries also provide *proof* that rejecting The System works. Their discoveries, breakthroughs and ability to influence people reveals the added power, insight, creativity and energy you gain once you have broken free. Therefore, you have nothing to fear. You are about to be given access to the knowledge that will make you ten times the person you once were. With it, you will be able to do anything, go anywhere and live exactly how you want to live.

Chapter 1

The Awakening: Your Journey to Greatness Begins . . .

One of the most memorable tales from the Bible is of Paul and his "road to Damascus" experience. In this story, Saul of Tarsus, a persecutor of Christians is on his way to Damascus with the intention of annihilating a Christian community. However, during this journey he is blinded by an incredible light and this, combined with a vision of Jesus Christ, has a profound impact on his outlook and beliefs.

Saul is affected so deeply he sees the error of his ways and converts to Christianity. Changing his name to Paul, he then goes on to redeem his sinful past by spreading the word of God and helping the people he once persecuted.

Paul's experience was an awakening, literally transforming him into another person. Although there were no blinding lights or voices from the heavens, the revelation I experienced in my last year at university was, in hindsight, very similar. A quantum shift in my mental and spiritual landscape, I found myself unable to go back to being the person I was. It was as if a light had been switched on and I'd reached a greater level of consciousness. With my horizons expanded, I could *feel* the reality of a greater life even though my circumstances were far from perfect.

Although this experience may sound grandiose, it's now my view such moments can be more common than you expect. Far from being the reserve of religious figures, they can be experienced by anyone who becomes alive to, or aware of, a different and greater way of living.

My own awakening provided me with the foundation for both this book and my life. At my lowest point, it cleared a path through all of my fears and self-doubt and struck me with a power that was undeniable. It's not often we can say that we are absolutely certain of something, but when I had this experience, I *knew* I had the answer to my predicament.

Now, many years later, it is time to share this secret with you. Although it may appear simple, this should not detract from its significance. What I'm about to tell you is both the antidote to a life devoid of meaning and the route by which you will fulfil all your potential. It changed my life. My hope is that it will do the same for you.

What I learned was this:

In order to escape a life of limitation, boredom and unhappiness, a person must commit themselves to the pursuit of personal greatness.

I suddenly saw that there was a big difference between just wanting, and actually *committing*. I had to commit to what I did want, not to what I didn't want. This meant giving free reign to my desires and dreams. Everything that inspired me, everything that made me feel alive and everything that I wanted to experience would propel me towards a future worth living.

The Pursuit of Greatness

Maybe the significance of this secret has not yet struck you. It wouldn't surprise me. At first, I was sceptical about the idea of pursuing greatness. Opening this Pandora's Box gave me visions of a life that seemed beyond my grasp and somewhat unrealistic. However, a strange thing happened when these thoughts flashed through my mind - *I started to feel great.*

From being a student who woke up numb with absolutely nothing to look forward to, I was beginning to experience a newfound energy. It was at this point that I understood the true power of the secret I had discovered.

Far from being unattainable, the pursuit of greatness was absolutely *fundamental* in giving me a new energy. Ironically, I needed something as grand as this to jolt me back to life.

To this day, I continue to use this revelation as guidance. It has taken me from being lonely, having no clue about my future, unable to support myself financially and experiencing deep seated self-doubt to finding love, being able to make a living through work I enjoy, having a lifestyle where I can set my own schedule, being happy and believing in myself. To say that it has transformed my life is an understatement. The power and inspiration it provides has enabled me to teach children who have gone on to play national level tennis, help countless clients give up smoking, lose weight, sleep peacefully and build self-esteem, and reach people from all over the world with my message about breaking free from The System. Although I'd be lying if I said my life has been without struggle since this revelation, because it forces me to look beyond my difficulties and connect with my higher purpose, I've always been moving forwards.

You too, will feel this profound impact as soon as you embrace the pursuit of greatness. Maybe you come to this moment with a total lack of enthusiasm for life, frustrated at a system that allows so few opportunities for true expression and adventure. Maybe you've got a point to prove, filled with potential but no apparent avenue through which it can be channelled. Whatever your circumstances, the old strategy of focusing on your issues and trying to deal with them one at a time *has* to stop. As of now, you don't give any mental attention to lower level issues. Instead, you get a dream, you get motivated and you start living up to the ideal of the person you want to be.

Making this apparently simple decision is the basis of lasting happiness. Why?

Because so much of life is dependent on focus.

Undoubtedly, you've heard about the power of positive thinking? Here's something they don't tell you. The relationship between thought and physical reality is *so* strong that you literally create your future through our thinking. Not God, not The System and not the environment you were born into - Just your day to day thoughts.

Therefore, the moment you make the pursuit of greatness your central focus, you immediately begin elevating both your mind and conditions. You'll feel happy because you're thinking uplifting thoughts and you'll remain happy because your environment will soon begin to change. It comes down to a simple choice - *stay in the light or stay in the darkness.*

As you begin your pursuit of greatness, though, there's something which you must be aware of. What you are doing is highly controversial. Inform most people you're following your dreams and they'll tell you you're playing with fire. It's a dangerous approach because we, and the world we live in, are imperfect. Therefore, no matter how hard we try, and no matter what measures we take, there is still a very good chance we'll fail in our pursuit of a greater life.

Then, what are we left with? Not only do we have to contend with the misery of living an incomplete life, we also have to cope with the disappointment of realising hope is an illusion. Instead, it's considered a much safer option to find a way to cope with your dissatisfaction. Learn how to subdue your discontent and accept life can never be how you want it to be. These strategies will take the edge off your suffering. You may have to water down your desires, but you'll escape the inevitable disappointment that comes from setting your sights too high.

This is The System's approach to dealing with your discontent. However, in a world where excellence is so highly prized, it won't reward you with anything above a mediocre life.

This is why I present the quest for greatness as the answer to all of your troubles. It encourages you to "think big" knowing this is the only way to develop the motivation needed to transform your life. It realises that *ordinary measures don't result in an extraordinary life*. To truly distinguish yourself you have to do the things other people are too afraid to do or too embarrassed to try.

You have now read the story of my awakening. As powerful as an awakening can be, though, it's just the start of the journey. Knowing there's a greater life does not automatically mean you can claim it. There is an important step you have to take before you can progress any further.

The Decision

You take the blue pill, the story ends; you wake up in your bed and believe whatever you want to believe.
You take the red pill, you stay in wonderland and I show how deep the rabbit hole goes.

- Morpheus (The Matrix)

These lines, taken from *The Matrix,* depict a moment in the film where the main character, Neo, has to make a life changing decision. Previously, Neo has been presented as a dissatisfied computer programmer. He lives his life alone and can't escape the feeling there's something wrong with "reality." These suspicions are confirmed when he's contacted by a band of freedom fighters led by a man called Morpheus. This man offers to enlighten Neo on his situation but before he can do so, Neo must make a choice between either a red or blue pill.

These pills represent two entirely different ways of life. If Neo chooses the blue pill, he will remain in The Matrix and forget he ever had an encounter with Morpheus. If he takes the red pill, then Morpheus will explain the secret behind The Matrix, and by doing so, reveal the cause of his discontent. In the end, it's his intuitive understanding that life in The Matrix is a mere shadow of how he could be living, that prompts Neo to take the red pill.

At present, you may feel like Neo. Frustration with life in The System has led you to this moment yet, at the same time, you may be apprehensive about the pursuit of greatness.

This is your dilemma. Knowing the path is not enough. You may have been awakened to the possibility of a greater life but will you have the strength to begin your journey?

This question becomes particularly poignant when considering that your awakening may not illuminate an easy path. In fact, it may lead you into direct conflict with our own "matrix" – The System. At this point, you'll have to decide whether the adversity you face is worth the potential payoff of a new, richer, more powerful life.

Neo had Morpheus to assist him in making this decision. This book is now your guide. Keep reading, and you will be strengthened to make the decision you must.

The Blue Pill

You are probably already aware of what taking the Blue Pill entails. This choice represents returning to The System. In some ways it's the easier option. The System will do everything for you and only ask for one thing in return – compliance. It will give you a job, a sense of security, a social life, a set of beliefs and even a personality. All of these benefits can be yours if you just agree to turn over the leadership of your life.

To some, this may sound quite appealing. A life where you don't have to think or act for yourself has its attractions. But what are the consequences of submission to The System? The following example, taken from Ross Heaven's book on Shamanism, *Spirit in the City*, explains:

At the age of 47, Simon was "Mr Reliable." He had worked for the same company for 20 years, been married for 25, and had two teenage children. He caught the 8.15 into town, the 5.15 home, always did his best, never quibbled about working late or on weekends when required to do so by his boss, helped his wife (who didn't work) with the housework, the children with their homework, and his elderly neighbour with her gardening and shopping on the modern and nondescript suburban estate where he had lived since getting married. He always seemed pleasant, if not cheerful, and was a quiet and undemanding member of the workforce in the executive offices of the food company where he worked in the finance department.

Some people are marked for attention within a

company; others strive to be noticed, to make their mark. Not Simon K. He had risen steadily through the ranks and been promoted when his seniors left, filling their place quietly and efficiently. Even when he spoke to his colleagues (which was rare) to check an invoice or on some other company errand, he was hardly even noticed. He was the last person anyone expected any trouble from. If he had an opinion on company policy (or any other matter), he kept it to himself and never rocked the boat.

Until one day when he came into the office at his usual time and then, crossing the floor, suddenly stopped and began to sob uncontrollably. His colleagues, stunned, were unable even to rise from their seats before the screaming began. As the first of them reached him, the second computer monitor hit the floor as he swiped it from the desk in front of him. He was dismissed later that day.

He had no idea what had overcome him, or why that day in particular but, as he spoke of his life to the therapist he later went to see, the pictured emerged of a deeply unfulfilled and unhappy man who had sacrificed his life to a job which was in no way involving for him, let alone enriching, and a lifestyle without adventure. His therapist worked with him for some months then, having some knowledge of soul retrieval, recommended him to visit my friend, which he did.

Normally, soul loss is associated with more dramatic causal events and so my friend had no experience of a case like this and did not at first recognise it as an example of soul loss. She decided to

27

attempt a Shamanic journey on Simon's behalf, however, and that proved the turning point in the therapy.

What she saw during this first journey was a small boy, the child of old – fashioned, almost Victorian, parents with a strong line in discipline, who was restricted in almost every normal boyish pursuit and punished severely for any transgressions. By the age of 10 he was a dour, plain and frightened child who had lost touch with every spirit of adventure within him – literally, for they had taken leave of him so that he could survive the stifling deep brown suffocation of his early years.

My friend began to recover these soul parts for him, in partnership with his therapist, who helped him to explore and re integrate these forgotten aspects of himself. Some months later, Simon was ready to return to public life. He has now set up in business for himself and relishes the thrill of the risks he takes every day. He has been reunited with his true spirit of adventure and is a fuller man and more at peace with himself as a consequence.[4]

This example provides a clear warning for anybody considering the "Blue Pill." A counsellor or psychotherapist might have claimed that Simon K. was suffering from depression. Although there were obvious signs that this was the case, I found the Shamanic explanation to be more appropriate. This describes Simon K. as having suffered a "Soul Loss" – a brilliant way of diagnosing the consequences of allowing The System to control your life. This "Soul Loss" left Simon K. completely numb and devoid of any impulse for adventure. He was living a reliable, routine life - an existence so out of harmony with his spirit that a breakdown occurred.

"Soul Loss" is the best way to describe this experience because Simon K. gave his whole life to The System. This is what he had been taught to do by his parents. He was raised to follow and comply and although this approach got him through childhood and some of his adult life, ultimately it failed.

This failure highlights something that a lot of people overlook when taking the "Blue Pill." Although The System provides comfort and the illusion of security, there are damaging, long term consequences of choosing this option. However, these consequences are subtle. Many people will not be aware of any damage occurring because the decay that The System inflicts is gradual. There will be no sudden disaster but over the years you'll notice a decline in your vitality.

Simon K. realised this, as his life became more mechanical than human. In the end, what appeared to be an extreme outburst was his soul's only way of fighting back. A similar outcome may await you, if you suppress your desire for greatness.

The Red Pill

The 'Red Pill' can be a deceptive option. The System often tricks us into believing that greatness can only be achieved by the lucky few. Portrayed as the reserve of the wealthy and famous, most people write off their prospects of living an extraordinary life. However, greatness can be achieved in a variety of forms and this common misunderstanding leads many to turn their back on what can be a surprisingly accessible path.

To make sure you're not one of them, you must undergo a change in perception. You must reject the notion that greatness can only be found through wealth or fame. Even when you hear stories of celebrities and entrepreneurs living lavish lifestyles and spending incredible amounts of money, you must not make assumptions. In fact, you must reject the belief that in order to be great; you have to follow in their footsteps. Above all, you cannot grant the famous or successful a status above your own. This will only result in naïve assumptions about how they were born that way or were incredibly lucky, both of which lead to beliefs disqualifying you from ever having what it takes to be great.

Once you have rejected this conditioning, you must then open your mind to the possibility that greatness can be achieved through *a determination to be yourself.* It's this stubbornness in not allowing your identity and dreams to be crushed that leads to an exceptional life. It's not about being born with incredible talent or benefiting from a stroke of luck. Instead, it's a quality within each person's grasp.

When taking these steps, it's important to remember that your call to greatness could be anything. It's doesn't have to be about changing the world or becoming a multimillionaire. As long as you have some great adventure that allows you to feel alive, then greatness is yours.

To demonstrate this point, we now turn to the story of Joseph Campbell. Campbell is probably best known for his writing (*The Hero with a Thousand Faces* 1949, *The Power of Myth* 1987) and influence in the creation of the original *Star Wars* films. However, his life encompassed many other areas including running (he set the New York City record for the half – mile) playing in jazz bands, studying at various universities and lecturing at Sarah Lawrence Women's College.

In his 20s, he rented a shack for virtually nothing and spent all day, every day, reading. His explanation? He was on a quest for knowledge. While most people would be terrified about how they were going to get by, Campbell realised there was something more important than making money to survive (he went without a job for 5 years). What mattered to him was the concept of "following his bliss."

This concept is virtually identical to the idea of pursuing greatness. It's about living a life that has the power to fascinate and absorb. Furthermore, it requires you to develop the strength of mind to resist The System's obsession with worrying about money or what other people might think of your seemingly weird lifestyle.

Campbell was able to do this and although The System might have ridiculed him for living in a shack and spending his days reading, it would be difficult not to agree he had the last laugh. Through embarking on his quest for knowledge, he was able to produce inspirational works that had an impact on millions. Furthermore, his ideas and philosophies, particularly his highlighting of the stages of the "Hero's Journey" in myth and literature (exemplified by the story of Luke Skywalker in *Star Wars*) have influenced and touched the lives of many people around the world. All of these achievements stemmed from an understanding that greatness is achieved through *following your bliss.*

This is the message *you* must take from his example. Campbell didn't become great because he was fantastically wealthy, famous or reached the top of the ladder. He didn't even become great through his achievements. What made Campbell great was a commitment to stay true to an exciting life philosophy. It may have led him in what many might consider an unconventional direction, but it was vital in unlocking his creative power.

To unleash your own, you must follow Campbell's example and resist making money, fame or power your main objective. An intense focus on any one of these may bring you success, but greatness will be beyond your reach. For this, you have to be involved with something you love and gets you really excited. Discard all notion of how big or small this project is, whether you're leading or playing a team role and especially, whether other people view it as important. Ironically, you may end up living a greater life by choosing a smaller project that has a much greater personal meaning, than pursing riches and discovering that for all your success, something is missing.

The Greatest

By choosing the "Red Pill," you are embarking on a quest for a greater life. However, in making this decision, you shouldn't fall into the trap of believing you have to know exactly where this path will lead. In fact, it's more than likely the path will be revealed *after* you've taken the first step. This means you can choose the "Red Pill" without having a clearly identifiable end point in mind. Such a decision is possible because greatness is achieved through *a commitment to excel in whatever you do.*

I first began to understand this point when I saw a television commercial featuring Muhammad Ali back in the mid-90s. In this commercial, Ali was questioned about what he might have done if he hadn't been a boxer. He didn't know but he was sure that whatever he chose to do, he'd have been "the greatest." Even if he was a postman, he said, he was going to be the best postman around, delivering the largest quantity of mail and therefore, becoming great.

At the time, I didn't fully understand the significance of the advert but I felt inspired. Just the conviction that Ali had in himself, that he was going to do and be something amazing, made me want to follow a similar path. He just had to express his desire to use and maximise his talents. He wasn't going to suppress this for anybody, and it's more than likely this attitude helped him reach the heights he did during his boxing career.

Ali's example demonstrates that greatness is not found after you've made your first million or through a significant victory. Instead, this quality is intangible. It's a burning desire to fulfil your potential that enables you to walk a higher path. Once you understand this, you can make your start. Ironically, this is usually all that's needed for a specific path or career to reveal itself.

When identifying this path, it's worth considering that today's spectrum of careers and jobs only scratch the surface of life's possibilities. A person should never doubt their ability to find a niche where they can put their talents to use. New professions, means of making money and ways of living are being created all the time. The world needs people who are prepared to take the 'Red Pill' in order to create this change.

* * *

You are now poised to make your decision.

This is your "Matrix" moment.

Take the "Blue Pill" and your life continues as it always has.

Take the "Red Pill" and you have a big commitment to make.

Inwardly you must commit to the ideal that you will stay true to yourself and accept the life you were meant to live. Such a decision is vital because it represents the first step. The journey can't begin until you mentally commit to seeing this through.

Not quite ready to make such a commitment? Understandably, nobody likes to make an ill-informed decision. The next section should go some way towards informing you on what to expect.

The Hero's Journey

Joseph Campbell has already been mentioned as a man who followed what The System would consider an unconventional path. As well as the concept of "following your bliss," he gave the world another insight into how to live a greater life. Through his analogy of the "Hero's Journey," he demonstrates that, if a certain path is chosen, everyone's life can become a great adventure.

Before creating this concept, Campbell spent many years reading and analysing ancient myths in search of a common theme. Once his reading was complete, he felt able to identify a few clear stages that became the "Hero's Journey." I present them to you now as they provide the perfect template on what you should expect when breaking free from The System. They are described here under their 3 main headings.

Stage 1: The Departure

The "Hero's Journey" begins with a "departure." This is the point where the Hero receives a calling to embark on an adventure with some specific goal or quest in mind. However, the Hero usually feels unprepared for this journey. They have become so accustomed to their quiet and unfulfilling life, they fear the prospect of change. As a result, they go through a period of soul searching before making the decision to tentatively advance.

Once this decision has been made, they must cross a threshold. This threshold represents the transition from their old familiar world of limitation, to the new, danger-ous but alluring world of their journey. To cross, they have to face a guardian who seeks to keep them within the confines of the life they used to know.

In the context of escaping The System, the "departure" relates to the first step in your pursuit of greatness. It highlights the difficulty that many people feel when breaking free from the life they know. There's a battle between desire and fear and sometimes the prospect of pain is a greater driving force than the potential for pleasure.

This is why you might experience a great deal of soul searching early on in your pursuit of greatness. It may even feel like this quest has been forced upon you. Unsatisfied with the life you have been living, yet fearful of what seems like an impossible journey, you feel damned either way. However, in these moments, it's important to remember what brought you to this point.

The restlessness of the life you've known *won't* go away until you heed its calling. Take it as a sign, prompting you to set your sights higher and pursue a course that's going to bring a *real* sense of meaning to your life.

Once you have committed to your own "Hero's Journey," your first challenge will be presented in the form of a threshold guardian. This could be at the point when you announce plans to set up your own business, quit your job or decide to retrain. Whatever your decision, it occurs at the very first sign of you acting in line with your new commitment.

At this point, The System will rear its head, acting through your friends, colleagues, parents and even your own doubts and fears. Attacking through words and thoughts, it will seek to influence you into believing that the journey you wish to undertake is fraught with hardship, or just plain impossible. Furthermore, it will play on the greatest of modern fears by portraying your quest as something that could leave you destitute and isolated from society.

Can you handle this barrage of negativity? The best approach to coping with this attack is to remind yourself of who is the ultimate arbitrator of your life. When it's all said and done, you only have to answer to yourself. Somebody may tell you you're crazy, but they're not you. They don't understand the desire burning inside you and nor can they appreciate the magnificence of what you want to achieve. Don't allow their limiting fears to become yours.

Stage 2: The Initiation

The second stage of the "Hero's Journey" is the "initiation." It is here that the hero must pass through a series of trials in order to achieve the object of their adventure. These trials usually test both physical prowess and spiritual development and their purpose lies in expanding the Hero's consciousness.

A classic example of this can be seen in, *The Matrix*, where Neo has to undergo a series of trials all aimed at altering his concept of reality. Morpheus oversees this training and is at pains to point out that Neo's ability and power is limited only by belief.

Star Wars also has a similar theme. When Yoda trains Luke in the ways of The Force, he's always stressing the importance of belief. It is through an understanding of this power that Luke is able to alter his notion of what's possible and unlock abilities vital for his future journey.

Freedom from "The Matrix" and mastering "The Force" are seen as the main objective of Neo and Luke's journey. In the "Hero's Journey," the achievement of your main objective is described as the "Ultimate Boon." This is the prize the hero has been working towards since the beginning of their quest. Once achieved it grants them access to a power that can change the world from which they came.

When it comes to escaping The System, the key message to be taken from the "initiation" is expect adversity. You will be tested to the limit because by rejecting The System you automatically remove yourself from the security it provides. As a result, you'll be on your own and, at least initially, will have to rely almost exclusively on yourself.

This may sound unappealing but there's an important point to remember when undergoing your initiation. It's only by walking a path that makes you experience hardship and pain you can develop the skills needed to rise above The System. The people who are afraid to test themselves are the ones who are powerless to break free. With this thought in mind, the numerous trials that are essential to achieving greatness become an opportunity for growth.

These trials will test you on a number of different levels. You'll need to develop the discipline to go the extra mile, the leadership qualities to convince others of your ideas and the resilience to overcome adversity. These are just some of the ingredients for greatness but the main challenge will present itself when *altering your perception of reality.*

To do this, your beliefs about yourself and life must change so that you can comfortably exist in a world where *anything* is possible. This altered state of consciousness could be described as the "Ultimate Boon." It blesses you with a mind-set that can rapidly change your life.

However, acquiring this power does not signal the end of your journey. To achieve greatness you need the courage to step back into the world you came from and use your power to shake up The System.

Stage 3: The Return

Once the Hero has passed through their initiation and acquired the "Ultimate Boon," they're faced with the prospect of returning to the world they used to know. This return is usually resisted. The grounds for resistance are based on the Hero feeling that he or she has either left their old world behind or that it could never understand or accept the new power and skills they now possess. However, if they are to complete their journey then they must return. It's only by applying their newfound knowledge they can find peace and permanently escape the unfulfilling life they used to know.

In the context of escaping The System, the "return" concerns the hero having the courage to put their talents to use. Often The System will make you feel reluctant to take this step for fear of ridicule or rejection. Since early childhood we have been programmed to fit in, conform and avoid expressing desires that seem far-fetched. As a result, a belief develops that individuality is something to be suppressed. We stick with what we know is acceptable and modify any behaviour that draws unwanted attention. Too fearful to pursue our dreams, we end up eaten away by our suppressed desires.

The solution to this predicament can be found in the pursuit greatness, but to complete this journey, a line must be crossed. This line represents the point where you decide to act upon your desires and by doing so, make a return to the life you were destined to live.

For this return to be successful, you'll have to confront one of your deepest fears. It's a fear that keeps many chained to The System but is not immediately obvious. In fact, it might appear paradoxical because it's not always our fear of failure that prevents us from putting our talents to use.

The counsellor and writer, Marianne Williamson, understood this well. She offers a brilliant explanation as to why so many of us resist allowing our talents and individuality to shine and in the process, condemn ourselves to a life trapped in The System. Her most famous quote explains all:

> Our deepest fear is not that we are inadequate. Our deepest fear is that we are powerful beyond measure.
>
> It is our Light, not our darkness, that most frightens us. We ask ourselves, who am I to be brilliant, gorgeous, talented, fabulous? Actually, who are you NOT to be? You are a child of God. Your playing small does not serve the world. There is nothing enlightening about shrinking so that other people won't feel unsure around you. We were born to make manifest the glory of God that is within us. It is not just in some of us; it is in everyone. As we let our own light shine, we unconsciously give other people permission to do the same. As we are liberated from our own fear, our presence automatically liberates others.'[5]

This view turns the nature of fear on its head. Williamson presents an opinion contrary to the accepted understanding of what holds us back. By doing this, she unlocks the main reason why the "return" is resisted. We are afraid of our own light because we fear that it will lead us into isolated glory. So long as we play small others will accept us because we share the common bond of mediocrity. However, as Marianne Williamson points out, this is not actually the case. In fact, we are all just waiting for someone to take the lead and demonstrate how to grasp a more meaningful life.

A Hero in The System

Discussion of the Hero's Journey and mention of myths may seem like a reality far removed from your daily existence. However, these stories were created precisely because they relate to the dilemmas and challenges that everyday people face.

In the past, myths were told as a means of inspiring people and creating a sense of wonder. Today, we receive our myths through films and books, with their power contained in their metaphorical meaning. You may not have to set out on a quest to find the Holy Grail or follow Morpheus into the world of The Matrix, but the struggles these characters face will shine a light on your own challenge to the way things are.

Joseph Campbell aimed to show it was not crazy to compare your existence to characters like Odysseus and Luke Skywalker – such archetypal figures could be reliable guides to what you might do in real situations, in your very real life. By seeing yourself in a similar way, suddenly, you are no longer Mr. or Miss Average. Instead, you're a potential hero, who has to face many trials and make great journeys both within and without. When understanding your life in this way you create a new level of excitement and by doing so, start to realise how it *should* be lived.

Before you embark on your "Hero's Journey," you must be aware that The System is quick to rubbish the value of dreams and myths. They're portrayed as little more than fantasy; a weak persons' means of escaping the demands of "The Real World." Yet we still have desires. We still have hopes and ambitions and perhaps if left to our own devices, we would live a more fulfilling life in the pursuit of these. However, we are not permitted to enjoy this kind of freedom. In fact, we are barely given a choice because from birth we have been influenced by a power that seeks to crush our desire for greatness.

It's now time to turn our attention to the exact nature of this power. You are about to discover the extent of The System's insidious influence. I reveal it to you now, because before you can hope to break free, you must first understand all the ways in which you've been constrained.

Chapter 2

The System: What it is and how it holds you back

You are a slave Neo. Like everyone else you were born into bondage, born into a prison that you cannot smell or taste or touch - a prison for your mind.

- Morpheus (*The Matrix*)

The System is intangible. It has no central location or power to make and enforce laws. Nobody works for The System and it will never directly compel you to do anything. Instead, it's a subtler power and rather than direct coercion, it operates through *influence*.

This influence is exerted through a belief system; a wide spectrum of ideas, opinions and thoughts that define our reality. You can hear this belief system expressed in the media, reinforced by your work colleague's, promoted by the government, accepted by your friends and imposed by your parents. It's the invisible net that, if we are not aware, can influence our understanding of life.

A few examples can be seen in the everyday assumptions we take for granted;

- Teenagers believing that if they're not out partying, getting drunk and experimenting with drugs then they don't "have a life."
- A belief that medical science is the only valid approach when it comes to healing and that any alternative is pseudoscience or new age nonsense.
- The notion that finding your purpose in life is secondary to living in "The Real World," paying the bills and holding down a regular job.
- The belief that it's normal to work for 40plus hours a week, for 40plus years of your life, often for nothing greater than financial reward.
- The idea that the individual is powerless to a make a difference to the world.

All of these assumptions (and many more) create boundaries in which we believe the truth about life to exist. From within these boundaries, little else seems possible or even plausible. As a result, our horizons shrink and our outlooks narrow. It's like we're living in The Matrix. Since birth, we have been *conditioned into accepting a false reality* and as a result, we are completely unaware that a different world could exist with endless possibilities for what we could be or do.

Of course, this system way of thinking gets updated and changes with time (go back two hundred years and it would have been a system belief that we originated from Adam and Eve) but the actual beliefs aren't the main problem. Instead, it's the assumption of truth. *It's the idea that the consensus majority opinion defines what can and can't be done, what is and isn't acceptable and what's cool and what's not.* Therefore, anything outside of these boundaries is feared, ridiculed or avoided, creating an immense pressure to conform.

Alongside The Matrix, the Overton Window provides another great analogy to explain The System. This concept, named after its founder, political theorist Joseph Overton, states there exists a window of politically acceptable ideas in mainstream politics. These ideas range from what is deemed "acceptable" to "sensible" to "popular" to finally becoming "policy." For example, today, in a modern western "democracy," it is taken for granted that capitalism is the only economic system that works, the market should be unregulated in order to enhance economic growth and that we need nuclear weapons as a deterrent against hostile nations.

Ideas outside the Overton Window, and therefore deemed "unthinkable," would be that humanity can successfully function without money, that we don't need armed forces or weapons as there is no enemy but ourselves and that economic well-being should be secondary to the well-being of the planet. These ideas, lying outside the Overton Window, get classified as extremist, dangerous, impossible and "what kind of planet are you living on" type thinking.

The Overton Window sets the agenda for what is

considered politically possible. By doing so, it forces politicians, and to a larger extent, the people, to conform to a set of trusted economic and political beliefs if they want to be taken seriously.

The problem is that these beliefs are not truths, merely just what happens to be fashionable at the moment, having proven some kind of worth in the past. As a result, the Overton Window halts humanities progress by narrowing the realms of political dialogue. All three of the ideas (listed above) would see a happier and healthier world, but because they're deemed "unthinkable" by those with the power to set the boundaries of political debate, are not even considered when it comes to creating policy.

The System, in comparison, is an Overton Window that stretches across all areas of life. Its belief net operates in the highest echelons of power, from Washington to Westminster, right down to the lowliest of ghettoes. Every environment and community has its system. For those in Washington, it's based on the dominant political ideas listed above. For those in ghettoes around Washington and elsewhere, it might be a pervading sense of hopelessness at ever escaping, and the limited outlook that dictates the only paths to doing so are through sports, possibly music and most likely, crime. Therefore, the most concise definition of The System I can give you is this,

The System is the dominant mode of thinking, or way of doing things, in whatever environment you inhabit.

This relates to your place of work, your school or university, your family and your church. All of them have a system

– *a set of written and unwritten rules about what is possible and acceptable* - and if you're reading this book, then I assume you want to escape.

But what does it mean to escape? Knowing you want to be free is one thing, knowing exactly what you need to be free *from* is another. **That's why it's so important to realise that escaping The System means freeing yourself from a mind-set that puts limits on your life.** For example, it means refusing to accept the only way to provide for yourself and family is by working a regular job which puts huge limits on your time, freedom and enjoyment. It means rejecting the notion that high levels of stress and struggle are a normal part of modern life and *have* to be tolerated. It means refusing to accept that you have to "play the game" in order to get ahead. And it could even mean refusing to accept the notion that we get old, our vitality decreases and eventually fall victim to some disease. You may want to escape all of these limiting assumptions and their manifestations in your reality. But, the question remains, what will you escape to?

This, my friend, I leave largely to you. While I can't talk about specifics, it's safe to assume you want to escape to a life of happiness, health, joy, freedom and one where you leave a positive mark on the world (greatness). You want to spend your days excited by the projects you're involved in. You want to live and work in environments that make you feel alive. You want to set your own working hours and control your time. In short, you want a life where you determine the terms for living it and don't have to play by anybody else's rules apart from the ones you willingly accept. This is what it means to escape The System. **First,**

you free yourself from its limiting mind-set and then you create a life where you do exactly what you want to do, when you want to do it.

The System creates its boundaries through social conditioning. From an early age, we're barraged with information and opinions about life and our role within it. Inevitably, as we develop, we begin to accept part of this belief system and define ourselves through it. This process continues well into adulthood until we reach a point where we believe our understanding of the world to be complete. When this occurs, the conditioning process is cemented and our outlook becomes fixed. The consequences of this are twofold.

Firstly, we accept The System's perspective. We begin to define our capabilities and understand life's potential according to this narrow set of beliefs that we've been conditioned to adopt.

Secondly, we become so dependent on The System for our sense of identity and security, that we'll fight any person or group that challenges its authority. Evidence of this can be seen on both a macro and micro level. A classic example is major institutions, like the media, mobilising against an individual or minority group. Perhaps the individual is about to reveal information that will expose the inaccuracy of The System's world view (Charles Darwin and the *Origins of the Species*). Or perhaps, in a fight for their rights, they refuse to be intimidated by the apparent invincibility of The System (Nelson Mandela and the ANC's struggle to end apartheid). Whatever form the challenge takes, people and institutions will always seek to suppress ground-breaking ideas and exciting new movements because their existence is an uncomfortable reminder they don't possess a monopoly over the truth.

To deal with this threat, The System will *come alive* within the people who believe their understanding of the world is being attacked. When you have several institutions (government, media, big business etc.) united by a single cause, the result is powerful. Discrediting, censorship or ridicule is the most common form of attack. However, in more extreme cases, physical violence and imprisonment are used.

On a smaller scale, The System comes alive in everyday people who feel their understanding of the world is being challenged. For example, your new business idea challenges a close friend or colleagues system influenced beliefs about what is possible. It might even expose the neglect of their dreams. Expect opposition from these people. They need to defend The System to defend their worth. Even if it means supporting a set of beliefs that limit their potential, they'd rather do this than have your potential success threaten the excuses they use to hide their own denial.

To some, these examples may appear to present a rather extreme, even paranoid analysis of how The System operates. In your quest for personal greatness you may have no intention of challenging the government or any vested interests. You are probably not interested in conspiracy theories. However, you need to be aware of the potential for influence The System has on your mind.

Its all-pervasive belief system represents a ceiling that any person seeking greatness must break through. This is the real relevance of The System in your daily life. It's the ease with which you can be subtly influenced into *accepting a pre-packaged life with stifling limits on your potential.*

The Maverick Doctor

The "Ultimate Boon" of breaking free from The System is the opportunity it creates. Detach yourself from its way of thinking and your consciousness becomes elevated above the ordinary. Instead of tuning into a narrow spectrum of how life can be, you are open to a whole universe of ideas and inspiration. Furthermore, you are immediately granted the impetus to pursue your dreams because you now believe in a world where anything is possible. It all comes down to this. Without that 'system voice' telling you what you want is either unachievable or unacceptable, there is so much more that you can do or be.

This freedom to go for what you *really* want should immediately appeal to anybody who is dissatisfied with life in The System. However, there is a common misconception that could cause you to turn or falter at the start of your journey. What you must realise is this:

Escaping The System does NOT have to mean complete physical separation from the world around you.

You do not need to quit your job, become a hermit and live in the woods. The error in this way of thinking is to see The System as a physical construct rather than an invisible net. What you are seeking to escape is not so much your job (although this could happen with time), paying the rent, mortgage, taxes and uninspiring people, but *an attitude* that accepts life as it has been presented. Therefore, *you can remain mentally outside The System while physically working your way through.*

This insight is the key to escaping The System. Isolating yourself from society is not always the answer. Sometimes, you have to shake it up. This could mean operating within it by pursuing your unique goal or mission that pushes its boundaries, while remaining mentally untouched.

Performing such a juggling act may seem impossible. However, it becomes easier when you remember all you have to do to escape the mental inertia of The System is to *find your own answers.*

It's this determination to heed your inner voice and not allow the conditioning of The System to influence you in any way which permits you to experience the magic of an unconstrained consciousness. Whether this leads you into the woods alone or sees you remaining in your present line of work is irrelevant. A mind untouched by The System's way of thinking will always be directed to a course of action that brings freedom and excitement into your life.

A man who personifies the idea of having to remain physically within The System (at least at the start of his journey) while mentally without, is Dr Hunter "Patch" Adams. His true story was made famous by the 1998 film, *Patch Adams.* This documents his struggle with the medical establishment as he sets up a practice on the grounds of treating patients with humour and compassion.

The real-life Patch Adams graduated from High School in 1963 and then went through years of medical training to earn his Doctor of Medicine Degree in 1971. Throughout this time, and even before, he was developing his own philosophy on how to treat patients. In essence, he believes in a more compassionate, holistic approach to health care. He's against health insurance and feels the health of an individual cannot be separated from the health of their family, community and the world at large. Furthermore, he urges medical students to develop compassionate relationships with their patients, believing that humour and play are essential to physical and emotional health.

With such an outlook, Patch Adams was always going to find it difficult to work within the medical establishment. Therefore, in 1971, he set up the Gesundheit! Institute which acted as a free community hospital for 12 years. He has also worked as a social activist, written books and organises volunteer expeditions to help orphans around the world.

I've included his example to demonstrate that you can still escape The System while working, what many would consider, a mainstream career. In fact, some of the most urgent changes the world needs to see can be found at the heart of The System.

- We need politicians who tell the truth instead of being evasive in an attempt to protect their electability.
- We need medical professionals who refuse to submit to the pressure to run a hospital like a business and instead, put their patients first.
- We need teachers brave enough to develop brilliant, independent thinking students rather than submit to the institutional demand for improved league table results.

- We need journalists who want to expose the truth rather than promote the newspaper owner's agenda.
- We need policemen and women who are genuinely driven to protect the people instead of making pointless arrests to ensure they meet government quotas.

Don't assume the anti-system sentiment of this book prevents you from working in these fields. Being true to our ideals, and conscience, is a path available to everyone, no matter where it leads.

Challenging The System: The Story of Galileo

Throughout this book, you'll read stories of hypnotherapy clients of mine who came to see me with various issues. They were people who could be said to live within The System. Some were lawyers, others students and some worked in the business world. However, this didn't prevent them benefiting from insights that were beyond the realm of The System's wisdom. In fact, many of them found their lives changed through following an approach that countered the way they'd been conditioned to deal with difficulties.

Just like my clients, *you* can also benefit from expanding your consciousness and leaving The System's way of thinking behind. In doing so, perhaps you'll now understand you're not embracing a conspiracy theory or an attack on capitalism. The System existed many hundreds and thousands of years before such ideas came into human consciousness. Perhaps it even stretched back to our Neolithic beginnings with unfounded superstitions that dictated what individuals within a tribe could or couldn't do. Whatever the case, it was certainly around 400 years ago in the time of Galileo. He waged a lengthy battle with The System that highlights both how it operates and why it's so important to challenge its horizons.

Galileo was an Italian physicist, mathematician, astronomer and philosopher born in 1564. His achievements in the field of science were vast. Sometimes known as "The Father of Modern Science" he made the first systematic studies of uniformly accelerated motion (now taught in most schools), improved telescopes, analysed sunspots and most famously, discovered evidence to support the theory that the Earth travelled around the Sun.

In 1632, Galileo's book, *Dialogue Concerning the Two Chief World Systems,* was published. In this book, he outlined evidence challenging the established system truth the Earth was fixed and the centre of the Universe (a belief promoted by the Church, based on scriptures in the Bible, and almost entirely accepted by European society). Such a challenge sent tidal waves throughout The System. The validity of its main institution - The Church - was being questioned and perhaps undermined. If Galileo's views were to spread then its authority could come into question.

Faced with such a challenge, The System (in the form of important members of the church) attacked, ordering him to appear in front of the Inquisition and finding him guilty of vehemently suspect heresy. As a result, he was forced to recant his views, placed under house arrest and received a ban on the publication of his book.

With such a crushing verdict, it appeared that The System had won and another lone voice had been silenced.

However, the word was out and although The System's truth was not immediately discredited, a few minds had been sparked by the idea there might be another.

Sowing such seeds in the consciousness of humanity is how The System's authority is undermined. It took time, but over the subsequent decades more and more people began to reject The System's truth that the Earth was the centre of the universe. Eventually this groundswell of consciousness reached such a level that in 1741, Pope Benedict XIV authorised the publication of Galileo's once heretic book. Then in 1835, all traces of opposition to heliocentrism (the term used to categorise those who believe the Sun to be the centre of the universe) disappeared from the church as further books were dropped from their banned index.

Such an outcome cements Galileo's place as one of history's greats. Although the view he promoted was not fully accepted until many years after his death, he played a significant role in advancing the collective knowledge of humanity. In doing so, he undermined the Churches ability to set the boundaries of reality - If they were wrong about the earth being the centre of the universe then they could also be wrong about other dictates that governed the way society operated. This trend has continued and the Church is now in a far weaker position today than it was in the time of Galileo. Over the centuries, many of its core beliefs have been challenged and, as a result, The System has had one of its arms removed.

Armless or not, though, The System still has power and as long as people continue to defend the dominant worldview simply because they've been conditioned to believe it's true, then it will continue to exist. However, for every individual that refuses to accept The System's reality and instead, pursues their own, its strength is diminished.

Perhaps humanities ultimate destination is a world where there are no boundaries to what can or can't be done. A place where there is no defined notion of what reality is and some of the mystery, excitement and adventure of life can be restored. Getting to such a place would see the emergence of a race of people able to maximise their potential. If they could point to their forefathers, the ones that led the way, they would identify Galileo. He demonstrates how far an individual can go when they refuse to accept The System's notion of the truth.

If he'd possessed the kind of mind accepting of the idea that the Earth was the centre of the Universe, then none of this would be possible. He simply wouldn't have looked for answers in places where he'd been told they didn't exist.

Such a possibility carries important implications for *you*. It raises the issue of how much *you'll* be able to achieve when unplugged from The System. Research claims we only use one tenth of our minds potential. Could this be the path to accessing those illusive nine tenths?

It's not altogether unfeasible. After all, a great chunk of us dies when conditioned to believe life can only be a certain way. Why do we need our full potential when it appears the opportunities for our lives are so limited?

We don't. We only need one tenth to operate in The System. However, when you believe in a world where no idea is off limits, you suddenly need those extra nine tenths. Your horizons have expanded, and to flourish in this new reality, so must you.

The System Strikes Back

Although the rewards of escaping The System are great, it's not always easy to break free. Throughout our lives a battle is being waged for the ownership of our minds. On the one side, we have our dreams and desires, urging us to live a life in harmony with who we truly are. On the other, we have The System, which influences us to suppress our individuality and pursue a life in line with the dominant expectations of the day.

You might think your instincts are the stronger of the two forces. However, this is not always the case.

The System is so effective at conditioning our minds because it catches us unawares. We don't even know what's happening and yet our lives are slowly becoming less and less about what we *want* to do, and more about what we *should* be doing.

This situation occurs as a result of a subliminal two-pronged attack. From an early age we are influenced by both the pressure to conform and lulled into an apathetic state known as The System's trance.

The Pressure to Conform

You go to school one day and realise that you don't fit it. The kids you used to be friends with all dress a certain way and have adopted new habits. Many of them smoke and drink and some have even started to experiment with drugs. Only a few of years ago you were at their house, playing football and exploring in the woods. You shared good times together, laughed and had fun.

However, now the game has changed. It's no longer about having fun. Instead, it's about being cool and appearing grown up.

Such a transformation leaves you in a dilemma. On the one hand, you want to have friends. You used to have fun with these kids and have many fond memories of growing up together. However, on the other, you have no interest in getting involved with their new way of life. The idea of smoking or taking drugs disgusts you and you can't see why it's so important you all wear the same style of clothes.

Stuck, you ponder your options. Be true to how you're feeling but risk the possibility of becoming an outsider? Or, suppress your feelings and adopt the lifestyle of your peers?

Although hypothetical, this dilemma is experienced by millions of teenagers at some point during their adolescence. At this stage, we become more aware of the world around us and anyone who doesn't appear to fit in. As a result, there is a pressure to become a part of something and a fear of being alone.

While, during our tribal beginnings, this fear served to protect us, there's a flip side to seeking safety in numbers. To really fit in with a group, or society, you have to follow the trends and adopt the behavioural patterns, attitudes and appearance of the rest of the collective. This plays right into The System's hands because, in the process, your individuality gets smothered.

This is how the pressure to conform leads and keeps us locked into The System. An instinct designed to protect us many thousands of years ago, drives us to seek safety through a group identity, having the adverse consequence of chaining us to a limited worldview.

Of course, we don't sign up knowingly. It just seems like the only feasible option. We're teenagers at the time and have little understanding of what's driving us to make the decision or where it will ultimately lead. All we know is that the other choice, of facing the world alone, is too terrible to contemplate.

This fear continues, and possibly even strengthens, as we reach adulthood. Now, facing the world alone could lead to a loss of income, a lack of romantic options, poverty, as well as social exclusion and the prospect of general ridicule. This pressures us to delve even deeper into the need to be protected by a group identity. We'll sacrifice even more of our desires and dreams and accept the majority view just so long as we don't have to be alone.

At this point, we're firmly embedded in The System. We've rejected our individuality to such a degree we don't have anything to provide a foundation for our lives. Instead, we have to accept the dominant view and belief system of our group or society, placing our destiny firmly in The System's hands.

A Story of Conformity

Talking in general terms about the pressure to conform is informative. However, specific examples of how it keeps people locked into The System will enable you to draw parallels with your own life.

What follows is one such example. It focuses on the

story of John (name changed for confidentiality), a hypnotherapy client of mine whose insomnia revealed an internal battle being played out between The System's expectations (represented by his father and peers) and his own desires.

When John came to see me, he'd been experiencing insomnia for almost a year. It developed gradually at first, affecting him only once or twice a week. However, as the weeks progressed, the frequency of the restless nights increased and it wasn't long before he had to function on only four hours sleep a night.

The pattern of his insomnia was excruciatingly predictable. Every evening he would fall asleep quickly, only to wake during the night and then find it impossible to return. From about three in the morning he would toss and turn, desperately trying to get back to sleep. He was rarely successful, though, and after only a few weeks of enduring this pattern, he found himself becoming depressed and lacking the energy needed to perform at work.

This bothered John greatly, both on a personal and professional level. At home, he was ill tempered and uncommunicative towards his wife. At work, in a highly competitive law firm, he felt his ability to excel in his field was being affected.

In this tired and frustrated state, John sought my help. Knowing that insomnia is usually a symptom of a much deeper issue, I asked him to tell me about his background. John told me about his childhood. From an early age, the idea of having a successful career in law had been instilled in his mind. He'd been pressured to excel by his father and his studies took up so much of his energy, he had little time for anything else. The bigger picture was always getting to an elite university to study law. From there, his father would use his connections to secure John a place at a prestigious law firm and a highly successful career would ensue.

With a keen intelligence and a titanic work ethic (forged by his father), this goal was achieved. However, it was at university, when free from his father's influence, that John was granted the opportunity to pursue his one interest outside of academics and law – art.

Throughout school, he'd excelled at this subject and displayed a natural aptitude that won him several awards. Now, John rekindled this interest by enrolling on extra curricula courses and painting in his free time. It wasn't long before he found himself immersed. When working on a picture he felt engrossed and completely occupied with his creation. By comparison, law was something dull and flat. He was so used to the grind of sifting through law books, he couldn't remember whether he felt any real passion for the subject.

With these doubts, John faced a dilemma. He entered his final year at university pursuing his passion for art alongside law. However, if he was to achieve the first-class honours degree that his father expected, something had to give. He couldn't spend a large amount of time painting and still achieve an outstanding degree. In fact, he would have to shelve his hobby completely. The demands of his course were simply too great.

The potential of making such a sacrifice had a deep impact on John. He began to experience sleepless nights as the stress of the situation took its toll. After re discovering the great passion of his life, he now faced the prospect of losing it. On the other hand, if he continued, he realised he'd be jeopardising a future he'd been pursuing his entire life.

He would think of these outcomes as he lay sleepless in his bed. In an attempt to gain clarity, he decided to talk to his parents and friends.

Predictably, his father disapproved of giving anything less than a hundred per cent commitment to his course. He then flew into a rage when John explained he'd been considering pursuing art as a career. He bluntly told John there was no money to be found in art. Law, on the other hand, was a much safer and more respectable option. He reminded John he'd been working his whole life to get to this point and to throw it away now was tantamount to wasting all of those years. To make his case complete, he then told John that he'd receive no financial assistance if he went against his wishes. He'd have to make it on his own.

John's friends painted a similarly bleak picture. They warned him about the years of poverty and hardship he would have to endure whilst establishing himself as an artist. To them, it seemed far too great a risk, especially when a successful and lucrative career as a lawyer was well within his grasp.

Without any input to the contrary, John found it hard to resist these opinions. He had frequent visions of failure whenever he contemplated becoming an artist. It seemed much easier to stick with the hassle-free life that law presented. He might have to endure long hours working in a job he found relatively dull, but this seemed more acceptable than the risk of pursuing his passion. In the final analysis, he felt he had gone too far down the road to becoming a lawyer. It made no sense to turn back now.

Despite the inner turmoil that John experienced, once he made his commitment to law, he never looked back. He completed his degree and began working in a prestigious law firm. Once there, he went from strength to strength, taking on important cases and being financially rewarded for his efforts.

John never thought twice about his dream of being an artist until the sleepless nights returned. This time, they appeared to be triggered by the news that his wife was pregnant. Although overjoyed, he knew it equated to added responsibility which meant a further commitment to his present career.

This was something he'd never questioned since his university days. However, now, he was forced to look at the bigger picture. He could quite easily continue to work in law until the age of retirement but that would mean forgoing any other ambitions. Ironically, it seemed he was faced with the same dilemma he experienced at university.

Although John could see the similarities between his current predicament and the one he experienced fourteen years ago, the side of him that yearned to be free from his father's wishes had been all but silenced. Years of conforming to his father's expectations, and the acceptance that his desire to paint for a living was just a fanciful dream, had left him with little appetite for turning his back on the life he had grown into. Besides, he hardly ever painted now and wouldn't know where to start. All his friends worked in similar fields and the path they all followed appeared to be the only one available. That was life to them. The necessity of surviving, and then being successful, meant they had to work their well-paid jobs whether they had any passion for them or not.

With the acceptance of his father's and friends' expectations, I felt that there was little I could do to help John. He could see that the insomnia was caused by his inner turmoil but was unwilling to explore anything that would challenge his current path. He saw that approach as the start of a very slippery slope and believed the stakes were too high to do anything but continue with his present course. Any return to the dreams of his youth could see him losing his finances, friends, security and even his wife. As a result, he asked me to stick to relaxation techniques and anything that would help him reduce the feelings of stress.

Reluctantly I agreed, and surprisingly, the outcome was more positive than I imagined. Although John's sleep was still disturbed, he did manage the occasional night where he slept all the way through. However, I felt this improvement would not be permanent. The part of him that was desperate to *live* would *have* to be expressed in one form or another. John could either choose to listen to it and take on board the lesson it was trying to communicate. Or, he would have to continue treating the symptoms of his unrest, hoping his insomnia wouldn't grow to the point of being unmanageable.

There are many lessons to be learned from John's story. Perhaps the most poignant is how the pressure to conform can cause a person to turn their back on what inspires them. When you have so many voices telling you to stick with what's safe, do what you're expected to do and not to rock the boat, taking any other course of action can appear overwhelming.

This was exactly how John felt. **It wasn't that his dream of becoming an artist was unachievable.** Rather, it was the pressure of his father's and friends' opinions that prevented him from finding the resources needed to make it happen.

This is why, whenever he visualised life as an artist, all he saw was a picture of poverty and struggle. In effect, *the pressure to conform cast a veil over a part of his mind.* It blocked out all of the thoughts and inspiration that could have helped him realise his dream. Instead, all that was left were images filling him with a fear that compelled him to conform.

By succumbing to these expectations, John demonstrated how the pressure to conform plays into The System's hands. It closes off the possibility of there being anything outside The System's reality. We shun anyone who's different, are fearful of expressing new ideas and are overly concerned with "fitting in." The pressure to conform acts as The System's prison guard. As soon as you pursue a course of action that challenges the status quo, it trains a rifle on you ready to fire.

Ironically, though, the rifle only fires blanks. If you were to step across The System's boundaries there's nothing the pressure to conform can do. Like The System itself, it's intangible and carries no *real* power. The threat is only in your mind, and if you can remind yourself of this and ignore all of the scared voices telling you not to cross the "shooting line," you'll discover that you can prosper on the other side.

Beating Conformity

So what? So what? I ain't got to be what nobody else wants me to be and I ain't afraid to be what I wanna be.

- Muhammad Ali (*Ali*)

Muhammad Ali is one of the 20th Century's great non – conformists. From his radical conversion to the Nation of Islam, and subsequent name change, to his refusal of the draft, Ali was never afraid to stay true to who he was.

In the above quote, from the film *Ali*, we hear him react to the furore created over his decision to refuse the draft. At the time, his comments sent shock waves through America. Here was no left-wing hippie, but the world's number one sports star denouncing the governments' policy. Many people may have shared Ali's sentiments, but nobody was supposed to express them (let alone in public, to a journalist!). Instead, in a time when the Cold War was on-going, every American was supposed to demonstrate their patriotism and desire to fight the scourge of communism.

Ali questioned this assumption, and coupled with his conversion to the Nation of Islam, this made him a figure of hate amongst many Americans. However, as the times changed, this hatred has transformed into an almost universal love.

He is now revered as a hero - a man who was able to transcend sport and touch the lives of millions. How did this transformation occur? Ali's comment, in the dialogue above, holds the key. In this scene, he is talking with his associates about his decision to refuse the draft. He has just given a reporter a highly inflammatory comment, telling him; "*ain't no Viet Kong never called me nigger,*" and now his associates are panicking. They're petrified at the consequences of their friend expressing such a controversial view. He, on the other hand, says, "*so what?*" It appears he doesn't care.

Of course, it's unlikely Ali was never completely unaffected by the controversy he created. However, he realised there was something greater at stake than the repercussions of offending people and causing public outcry.

He knew that *if he didn't take a stand for what he believed in, then he could lose his identity.* As he says, "*I ain't afraid to be what I wanna be.*" It was this strength of character and refusal to sell his soul, no what matter the consequences may be, that eventually won him his undying support.

In gaining this support, he demonstrates that he is a level above some of today's sports stars and public figures. They are frequently seen making cowering public apologies because they are so terrified of damaging their careers or marketability. Ali refused to give in to this fear and faced the prospect of reprisals head on. He knew full well that his stance could result in him spending 5 years in jail or, at a minimum, being banned from boxing during his prime. However, he stood his ground. Such bravery sets an example for anybody who seeks their own share of greatness.

Ali's attitude towards the prospect of reprisals represents the best way to beat conformity. To all the people who ask you "What will people think?" and to that inner voice that forces you to dilute your behaviour and actions for fear of criticism, there must be only one response – *so what*!

Such a strong response is necessary because there's a lot more at stake than the prospect of embarrassment. *The suppression of your spirit could occur.* Although this consequence may not appear as immediate as the criticism of others, or the disapproval of those you considered friends, it can have a much deeper and lasting impact through the eventual loss of your identity.

If this occurs, you'll become a puppet for The System, spouting out a string of ideals and opinions that you've been taught to believe in. All the while, your true desires and the *real* direction your life was meant to take will be ignored as you hide behind the apparent security of being one of the crowd.

Ali never sought this security. He wasn't afraid of who he was, and this individuality eventually captured the hearts and minds of millions. You could take similar steps but to do so, *you must not be afraid of being yourself.* In a world where so many people are, to find someone who isn't, is a genuine hallmark of greatness.

The System's Trance

We believe that our reality is *the* reality, but is it?

Steven Wolinsky's work suggests otherwise. While most people would see a hypnotherapist to be hypnotised, Wolinsky operates in a different way. He understands his role as being one of *dehypnotising* his clients. This approach is outlined in his book, *Trances We Live*, which explains his theory that most people spend their days in a state of trance. The nature of this trance will shift (from a day dreaming about the past trance, to a day dreaming about the future trance, to a car driving trance, to a social interaction trance etc.), but the key idea is that we spend our lives on autopilot, locked into a habitual state of mind. As a result, when we slip into a problem state (which could range from a smoking trance to an anxiety trance) we are, in effect, unable to *awaken* from our issue. This is why Wolinsky understood his role as being one of dehypnotising his clients. He would use his skill as a therapist to interrupt the client's problem state and thereby awaken them to a life without their issue.

Wolinsky's concept of the "trances we live" provides a brilliant way of understanding The System's influence over our minds. Trance is defined as the focus on one particular object whether internal (a certain thought) or external (e.g.; a television screen) to the exclusion of all other stimulus. Therefore, *The System's trance is the narrow focus upon a particular way of life, or belief structure, to the exclusion of any other reality or possibility.* Put simply, it's a state of mind that accepts life the way it is and therefore, leaves a person unaware of their ability to live a greater one.

If you wish to claim this greater life then you'd do well to follow Wolinsky's approach. He interrupted an unproductive mental focus and awakened his clients to the idea that there was life outside their issue. Switching from a focus on one particular way of life to an outlook where almost anything is possible, could also be the key to transforming your life.

When making this switch it's important to remember that it's about what you perceive as reality and what you believe is possible. Therefore, the broader your outlook, the more alive to certain possibilities and ideas you become. One of these possibilities or ideas might contain the keys to a greater life, but you must be open to it. Spend your days accepting everything you are taught and believing life can only be a certain way, and you might never awaken to the possibility of greatness.

Awakening from The System's trance is not easy though. Being permanently *distracted* from the possibility of greatness is a natural reaction to living in The System. It comes with the territory. Live by its rules and you have no grand dream, guiding principle or foundation upon which to build your life. As a result, you leave yourself open to being controlled by somebody else's agenda.

The possibility of this occurring makes taking charge your daily thoughts of paramount importance. Are you directing them towards a higher purpose (a greatness trance) or do they just wander, orchestrated by the events of the day (The System's trance)? It may seem a simple step, but this daily discipline will revolutionise your life. Constant thoughts of goals you want to achieve and experiences you wish to enjoy put you in the best possible state to make them happen.

You are Getting Very Sleepy

Taking ownership of your thoughts could be one of the most important steps you ever take. Not just for what it will help you achieve, but, also, for what it will save you from. There are two ways we get lulled into The System's trance and you must be aware of them both.

Firstly, The System provides us with all the answers we need to operate in its reality. Everything can be explained by scientists, the media, teachers and our parents. There's no land that hasn't been explored, there's no phenomenon that a scientist can't write a formula for and there's no other way through life apart from the one our parents and peers have followed. As a result, we become closed to the mystery of life. We inherit a pre-packaged world where everything can be explained and life's possibilities are already marked out.

The outcome of this inheritance is that our questioning faculty becomes diminished. We are taught to follow and accept rather than think for ourselves and question. This is what lulls us into The System's trance. It relates back to those inactive nine tenths we fail to access. We don't have to find a direction for our lives. We don't have to find answers. We don't have to face challenges on a daily basis. As a result, we don't need to be that focused. The System will do it all for us just so long as we turn up and play by its rules.

Information overload is the second stream through which we get sucked in The System's trance. Magazines, newspapers, internet, I Pads, mobile phones, computer games, YouTube, Facebook, advertising, radio stations and TV with hundreds of channels, make it all too easy to remain in a permanent trance like state. We can just skip from one information stream to the other and avoid that inner voice asking those inconvenient questions about who we are and what we are here to do.

Avoid these questions, though, and you might find your life becomes a surface level experience. You wake up in the morning, travel to work, do your job, return home, watch TV, go to the gym or meet friends and then to bed. This pattern could repeat itself for over 250 days of the year. You might have the weekends and holidays to add variety but as long as you remain on autopilot, you'll be prevented from reaching a deeper level of consciousness.

Accessing this level is fundamental to breaking out of The System's trance. Whether you partake in meditation, long walks, write in a diary or any other activity that gives you room for reflection, finding time to connect with your desire for greatness is vital. In doing so, you'll join history's greats who all shared one thing in common - *they were the masters of their minds.* At the forefront of their thinking was their life's purpose. This was never allowed to fade away for any substantial period of time and as a result, they were able to harness all of their mental and physical power when the time came to achieve their goals.

You must emulate these greats with a similar mental discipline. Don't allow a day to slip by when you aren't thinking about what you want to achieve and become. This practise elevates your consciousness above The System's trance and will eventually enable you to enjoy a life of freedom and greatness.

Escaping the System

Reasonable men adapt themselves to the world.
Unreasonable men adapt the world to themselves.
That's why all progress depends on unreasonable men.
                                        - George Bernard Shaw

The great set themselves apart by questioning what others take for granted. In contrast, most people accept what they are told and understand this as reality. Their role then becomes one of adapting themselves to this existence and doing the best they can to "get by."

The person who successfully escapes The System has a different take. They understand reality as something that should be moulded to their desires. To them, conformity is a sin and they hold onto their dreams without regard for external appearance.

Through their success, they reveal the true nature of The System. Rather than being an all-powerful force that defines the boundaries of human possibility, it is actually a powerless entity that exists only in our minds. The System's chief weapon in this grand illusion is the fear of what might happen. The media, the government, our work colleagues, and even friends and family, will present outcomes of disaster to anybody who strives for the seemingly impossible. However, without means of imposing its will, The System's threats are empty.

There is nothing chaining you to your present existence apart from the belief that change is impossible. Once you learn to understand your own role in the creation of your limits, you alight upon the key that will eventually set you free.

The next part of the book will instruct you on how to use this key. While my explanation of The System has been thorough, I've deliberately left room for you to apply your own intuitive interpretation to the concept. This understanding, typically gained through personal experiences of either being screwed, or oppressed, by The System, is vital in gauging what you want to break free from.

Perhaps you've given everything to the company you work for, only to find that, when the profits are down and they're looking to save money, they didn't think twice about letting you go. Perhaps you've lived your life abiding by every law only to be harassed by the Police and falsely arrested when protesting your innocence. Maybe you've saved your entire life, believing The System's economic logic is fundamentally sound, only to find that a financial crisis comes along and wipes out your investments. Or, maybe you're just sick of reading reports about how governments, corporations and the military, all spouting The System's doctrine that economic expansion is fundamental to the existence of the human race, set about destroying the planet and financing wars to ensure personal gain for a tiny percentage of the population. All of these experiences, and many more, cause the fires of injustice to rage in our souls. Until now, though, disillusioned and outraged as you are, you perhaps thought there was little you could do.

This is not the case. The subsequent chapters will reveal how to build a life untouched by The System. Furthermore, in doing so, you'll also develop the strengths, skills and wisdom, which should you choose to use; can be directed towards undermining The System's influence and building a freer, more compassionate world.

So, no matter what you're going through, or how far you feel you've fallen, *know* that there is a way out and that a fun, free and meaningful life is just around the corner.

Chapter 3
How to Find your Path through Life

So far, the pursuit of greatness has been presented as a way out of the soul crushing experience of life in The System. However, when attempting to break free, most people find themselves faced with a dilemma. Although carrying no great appeal, The System *does* provide structure, routine and a path to follow. Without this influence, who or what will be there to guide you?

Dissatisfaction with The System is experienced by the majority but there are far fewer voices presenting any viable alternatives. Greatness means different things to different people. There is no universal measure of what it means to be great and, therefore, no universally recognised path on how to get there. Instead, what you are left with is the initially uncomfortable prospect of *finding your own path.*

30-Year-Old Boys

Tyler Durden: *My dad never went to college, so it was real important that I go.*
Jack: *Sounds familiar*
Tyler: *So, I graduate, call him up long distance, I say, "Dad, now what?" He says, "Get a job."*
Jack: *Same here.*
Tyler: *Now I'm 25, make my yearly call again. I say, "Dad, now what?" He says, "I don't know, get married!"*
Jack: *I can't get married. I'm a 30-year-old boy.*

- Fight Club

In *Fight Club*, the main character, Jack, is deeply dissatisfied. He hates his job, is bored with his life and suffers from insomnia. Massively disillusioned, he wants to change but can't conceive an alternative to The System's path.

This path is revealed through a conversation he has with Tyler Durden (the films other main character and Jack's mentor). In this particular scene (see dialogue above) Tyler is talking with Jack about the advice his father gave to him on navigating his way through life. The conversation is one you are perhaps all too familiar with.

- You *should* go to college/university because it gives you the opportunity to get a good job.
- You *should* get a good job because that's how you make lots of money and gain respect.

- You *should* find a wife/husband and start a family because that's what everybody does when they've acquired a measure of stability.

This is the extent of The System's guidance when it comes to finding your path through life. It's based on societal expectations and is centred on how to gain a comfortable (but not a fantastic) amount of wealth, paint yourself with a veneer of acceptability and avoid any risk which might endanger the above. It teaches you to make important life decisions based on *the fear of what you might lose*. Follow it, and you *might* live a safe life, where your days are routine and largely predictable, but it can't offer you anything greater.

Unless you were fortunate enough to be blessed with exceptional parents and teachers, it's likely they'll have advised you to follow this path. They believe they're helping, being all too aware of the supposed dangers of life that the previous generation constantly warned them about, and feel they must counsel you in this time-honoured tradition. However, a lifetime doing what was expected of them has robbed them of their ability to dream and for this reason; you should NOT follow their advice.

I'd understand if you find what I've just written contro-versial, if not scary. Breaking free from our parents, teachers and peers' expectations can be one of the hardest steps we ever take. However, it is absolutely fundamental to your development and completely essential in equipping you with the strength and independence of mind needed to escape The System.

Failure to do so places you in the unfortunate category described by Jack as a "30-year-old boy." This ingenious term refers to generation of people (male and female) who seek security and comfort over adventure and self-discovery. Their life is little more than a copy of their parents and peers. They'll never experience the joy of succeeding in a field that they're genuinely passionate about and they'll never have a life changing impact on another person. Instead, their future could be accurately predicted for them by the time they reach adulthood. Following The System's path, the most they can hope for is material reward and the solace of their comfort zone.

If you find the prospect of being a 30-year-old boy unacceptable then you will have to abandon The System's path. This bold move does not have to be daunting. As always, you will have insights from those who have already forged their own paths to help guide your way. Read on to learn their secrets.

Be Inspired

God gave you the gift to sound like anybody you please - even yourself.

- Della Beatrice *(Ray)*

The above line is taken from *Ray,* an Oscar winning biopic about the life of the musician Ray Charles. The film follows his life, from a childhood where he loses his sight at the age of seven, to the point where he successfully overcomes his heroin addiction and cements his place as one of the twentieth century's greatest musicians.

Early on in the film, Ray has to find his own path. He's been enjoying some success mimicking other styles and singers but Della Beatrice (Bea, his future wife) challenges him to create something original. She likes his music but feels it lacks an edge. Ray agrees but at the same time is afraid of jeopardising the success he has fought so hard to achieve. However, ultimately, he realises that if he is to make the transition from good to great then he will have to bring something new and fresh to the world of music.

In the film, this moment is portrayed in a scene where he is lying on a bed with Bea. They are talking and suddenly he gets up and tells Bea that he wants to play her some music. What comes out of his mouth is the mixture of gospel and blues for which he would become famous.

However, Bea is shocked when she first hears this sound and declares it sacrilegious (at the time it was considered offensive by some to use church music in popular songs). An argument ensues where Ray tries to explain to Bea why it is that he's merging these two styles of music. He tells her that this merger is what comes *naturally* to him. He's been playing gospel and blues separately for his whole life and has a love for both genres. It just seems very natural for him to merge the two and express himself in this way.

The path that Ray Charles took to finding his own sound (and subsequently fame, wealth and critical acclaim) reveals a great deal about the path to greatness. It's interesting to note the word *natural* is used frequently throughout his argument with Bea. The inclusion of this word reveals something about the process he went through to discover his unique sound. It indicates that he allowed the sounds and styles that inspired him to *create* a direction he could follow. Even though he was looking for a breakthrough, it wasn't a case of deliberately planning to create something original. Instead, by working with what inspired him, he was *given* a sound and direction that enabled him to achieve greatness.

This process speaks volumes about what it takes to identify the path to greatness. It indicates that, when the time is right to make an important leap, it should feel very natural. Ray didn't have to force anything. In fact, the moment he stopped trying to force and be what he was not, was the moment he took the stabilisers off his musical career.

Previously, he'd grafted and imitated others to get a foothold in the music industry. However, when he realised that this could only get him so far, it was his ability to look within and *find out what it was that he really loved about his particular field* that facilitated a quantum leap in his career.

Something similar could be waiting to happen to you but to take this leap you must remember Ray's message. No path to greatness is ever found by imitating or forcing a direction. Instead, simply follow those abilities and interests that come naturally to you. Fall into it and let your path *emerge*. Even if it means you initially work for free or earn very little money, walking a path that comes naturally galvanises, you with an energy that will always create success.

This point must be remembered when you make those first tentative steps away from The System's path. The path to greatness is always in flux, meandering and changing along the way. Just because you start out small doesn't mean one day your natural love for what you do isn't going to create some opportunity or opening that you didn't previously see.

The Goosebumps

Another example from the world of music further elaborates on finding the path to greatness. In this case, the famous record producer and composer, Quincy Jones, discusses his involvement in the making of Michael Jackson's album *Thriller*. He explains his approach to the creative process below and in doing so, reveals a method for discovering your path:

> We got kind of trapped on Thriller because we had about 4 months to do it, which isn't a long time when you're following 10 million albums [referring to the sales of the previous Jackson album Off The Wall] because that stuff does affect your head.
>
> And there is no spiritual way to connect with saying, "Ok we're going to make a bigger album than that." You can't. You have to do something that gives you the goose bumps and say, "Yeah man, that really turns me on!" Because if you get turned on a lot, you got a chance of somebody else getting turned on.
>
> You still have to go with god's divining rod which is the goose bumps.[6]

Jones's comments refer to the importance of *feelings* when finding your path. He mentions it's impossible to find direction with an attitude that says, "*Ok, we're going to make a bigger album than that.*" This is an approach that focuses purely on outcome. It's an attempt to force out what you desire involving strain, effort and exertion. All of these qualities are the enemies of creativity and Jones realised *Thriller* would not be as great as it could if they took this approach. Therefore, they had to find a different strategy and what he presents is the logic free – and much more exciting – path to greatness.

This approach is guided by the idea of allowing the "*goose bumps*" to act as "*God's divining rod.*" When saying this, Jones means *he relies on his feelings for insight into which direction to take.* The reaction of "*getting the goose bumps*" to an idea or piece of music lets him know he's on the right path. He then pursues this path and allows the inspiration it generates to create an exciting new sound.

It's interesting to not Jones refer to "God's divining rod." What could he mean? Although this phrase may conjure up images of dowsing for water or metal detecting, you must take him seriously. His approach realises that you can't analyse your way to greatness. Your path through life is something deep and spiritual. Not in the sense that you become a priest, rabbi or even a guru, just that whatever you do must generate an instinctive buzz. Only this lets you know you're in touch with your true-life purpose.

Jones certainly struck gold when it came to making *Thriller.* He ran his divining rod over the hundreds of different ideas and songs that Michael Jackson and other songwriters and musicians presented to him. When those goose bumps hit him, he knew he was onto something great. The song or idea might need developing but it was that initial spark of excitement that provided the seed for a future masterpiece.

This method can also be used in *your* life. Whether its romance, guidance on a decision you have to make or a change of career, you must identify the source of your enjoyment and inspiration. Then don't be afraid to follow it. There may be a lot of fear and doubt surrounding the decision you want to make but you'll learn to trust your feelings. Combined with the other steps in this book, they'll never let you down.

At times this method may seem illogical but it's worth remembering that, when escaping The System, formulas and planning is often cast aside. This is because you're embarking on a journey that requires *passion*. It's not The System's path, where considerations of finance, acceptability and security need to remain at the forefront of your mind. Instead, it's a path that's walked with the freedom of a movie or novel.

It's important to note you won't always be able to sit down and calculate the likely outcomes of each step. Sometimes you have to go with what feels right. There may be no logical explanation and you may even appear to be confronting some form of danger, but you must remember those feelings are there for a reason. They give you the goose bumps because they contain a message. The excitement alerts you to the potential for greatness.

Following your Bliss

If the two concepts of doing what comes naturally to you, and using your feelings as a guide, could be packaged into an easy to understand message it would be this – *follow your inspiration*. This simple piece of advice has a life changing impact because it forces you to find a path that's guaranteed to stimulate. Gone are the days of dreading work and longing for the weekend. In their place is a genuine sense of purpose and fascination with all you do. What's more, there's no forced motivation. Instead, the drive to complete tasks, work on a project or go to work comes naturally because you're enjoying what you do.

Such an approach may sound too good to be true. It would be understandable to think that "following your inspiration" won't work in "The Real World." That's why I've included the next example. It focuses on two very real people who are discussing the impact of following their inspiration and how it has helped them navigate their way through life. Taken from the book, *The Power of Myth*, it features Joseph Campbell and co-author, Bill Moyers, discussing their version of the idea, which they call "following your bliss."

MOYERS: Do you ever have this sense when you are following your bliss, as I have at moments, of being helped by hidden hands?

CAMPBELL: All the time. It is miraculous. I even have a superstition that has grown on me as the result of invisible hands coming all the time – namely that if you do follow your bliss, you put yourself on a kind of track that has been there all the while, waiting for you, and the life that you ought to be living is the life you are living. When you can see that, you begin to meet people who are in the field of your bliss, and they open the doors to you. I say, follow your bliss and don't be afraid, and doors will open where you didn't know they were going to be.[7]

Campbell's life certainly validated this statement. He walked a path that gave little thought for The System's concerns yet was always involved with some exciting project and managed to achieve many goals. The most relevant point he makes when talking about "following your bliss" is it puts you on a track that has always been there. When this occurs, *"the life you ought to be living is the life you are living."*

What he's talking about here is a spiritual navigation system. You may believe such a thing could never exist but ask yourself this, "What's the purpose of my feelings?" Surely, they are God's, or whatever higher power you believe in, method of communicating with you. They teach you right from wrong and alert you to what's going to bring enjoyment into your life and what's not.

It's really that simple! The complication lies in The System teaching us to ignore and deny our feelings. Instead of using them, it wants us to plan and rationalise a situation.

This is all very well until you consider that The System's logic is totally f##ked up. Happiness is gained through the material. Respect is achieved through beating others. Peace is attained by buying yourself a vacation that lasts 2 weeks of an otherwise non-stop year. What kind of logic is that?

This is why we're left with no other choice but to follow our inspiration. Don't be the person who chooses a college or university course based on what they think is going to get them a job, marries someone because they believe that person will provide security or makes decisions based on what they fear losing. Be the person who never settles until they're completely satisfied with their life, pursues their passions without thought for how it's all going to work out and makes decisions based on what they stand to gain.

To locate your spiritual navigation system, you have to connect with something more than a desire to make money or an aspiration for a better life. It's deeper than that. Essentially, it's about reconnecting with the person you are meant to be and living the life you're meant to live. That's why the "hidden hands" emerge. Your feelings are a divine connection and being guided by them puts you in direct contact with your higher purpose.

This new understanding should give anybody who is struggling to find the path to greatness a sense of encouragement. It tells you that you are not alone. There is an invisible support system that will guide you. With its help, you *will* find a path and be that braver, wiser, more charismatic version of yourself. However, to get there you have to follow the signs.

You can't ignore or be afraid to act on your promptings, intuitions and visions. All along, they've been trying to communicate with you and tell you something that needs to be heard.

Ray Charles pursued a musical direction that came to him naturally. Quincy Jones used the feeling of goose bumps to let him know what was going to make a hit. Joseph Campbell followed his bliss. How do you know what inspires *you*?

The Eureka Moment

Developing an awareness of the interests, lifestyle and people that fill you with a sense of inspiration is the key to finding your path. Reconnecting with your feelings is the route by which this is achieved. Both gear you towards one all important moment.

The *Eureka Moment* was popularised by the tale of the ancient Greek scholar Archimedes. When he stepped into a bath and noticed that the water level rose, he realised the volume of water displaced must be equal to the volume of the part of his body submerged. Upon having this realisation, he proclaimed the word "Eureka," which means "I have found it."

Since then, the term has been used in connection with many great scientific discoveries. These discoveries are usually made in a moment of inspiration, when an answer or direction is revealed in an almost divine manner. Now you have committed to walking the path to greatness, you should be mindful of such moments. Although rare, they are of great importance. It's no exaggeration to say they are the cornerstones of your quest.

It may seem odd to think that you may have a Eureka moment very soon but you need to remember that the quest for greatness is no ordinary journey. It involves grand dreams and an unusual amount of commitment. Therefore, when an answer or direction that advances your quest comes to you, expect it to hit with a force that is undeniable.

As a result of this experience, you may be left with the vision of a goal you want to achieve or a field of work you wish to commit your life towards. On a lower level, it might provide you with an answer that will enhance your progress at work or further enlighten your understanding of life. In whatever way these eureka moments strike, they will be accompanied by powerful emotions. These act as an indicator. They make you aware something important is occurring and it would be wise to follow the path your answer reveals.

An Answered Prayer

Eureka moments happen to those who commit their life to the fulfilment of a grand ideal. Few have had worthier ambitions than Martin Luther King. His path to greatness involved fighting segregation in 50's and 60's America. His dream was to help build a nation where race was irrelevant and every citizen could enjoy the same opportunities.

Like most people who challenge The System, King's path was fraught with danger and hardship. Along the way, he faced violence, imprisonment and countless death threats. Such adversity would make even the strongest of men question the path they had chosen and Martin Luther King was no exception. However, it was at his weakest point he was hit by a moment that illuminated the path he had to take.

The following passage, taken from his autobiography, recalls this experience.

One night toward the end of January I settled into bed late, after a strenuous day. Coretta [his wife] had already fallen asleep and just as I was about to doze off the telephone rang. An angry voice said, "Listen, nigger, we've taken all we want from you; before next week you'll be sorry you ever came to Montgomery." I hung up, but I couldn't sleep. It seemed that all my fears had come down on me at once. I had reached the saturation point.

I got out of bed and began to walk the floor. I had heard these things before, but for some reason that night it got to me. I turned over and tried to go to sleep, but I couldn't sleep. I was frustrated, bewildered, and then I got up. Finally, I went to the kitchen and heated a pot of coffee. I was ready to give up. With my cup of coffee still untouched before me I tried to think of a way to move out of the picture without appearing a coward. I sat there and thought about a beautiful little daughter who had just been born. I'd come in night after night and see that little gentle smile. I started thinking about a dedicated and loyal wife, who was over there asleep. And she could be taken from me, or I could be taken from her. And I got to the point that I couldn't take it any longer. I was weak. Something said to me, "You can't call on daddy now; you can't even call on mama. You've got to call on something in that person that your daddy used to tell you about, that power that can make a way out of no way." With my head in my hands, I bowed over the kitchen table and prayed aloud. The words I spoke to God that midnight are still vivid in my memory:

"Lord, I'm down here trying to do what's right. I am here taking a stand for what I believe is right. But lord, I must confess that I am weak now, I'm faltering.

I'm losing my courage. Now, I am afraid. And I can't let the people see me like this because if they see me weak and losing my courage, they will begin to get weak. The people are looking to me for leadership, and if I stand before them without strength and courage, they too will falter. I am at the end of my powers. I have nothing left. I've come to the point where I can't face it alone."

At this point it seemed as though I could hear the quiet assurance of an inner voice saying: "Martin Luther, stand up for righteousness. Stand up for justice. Stand up for truth. And lo, I will be with you. Even until the end of the world."

I tell you I've seen the lightening flash. I've heard the thunder roar. I've felt sin breakers dashing trying to conquer my soul. But I heard the voice of Jesus saying still to fight on. He promised never to leave me alone. At that moment I experienced the presence of the Divine as I had never experienced Him before. Almost at once my fears began to go. My uncertainty disappeared. I was ready to face anything.[8]

Through his unbreakable faith and essential belief in the righteousness of his cause, Martin Luther King was able to influence the minds of millions of Americans. Laws were re written and attitudes changed and he is now heralded as one of the 20th Century's greatest leaders. None of this may have happened if he hadn't had his own Eureka moment in the small hours of that January night.

In this moment, King talks about seeing the "*lightening flash*" and hearing the "*thunder roar*" - metaphors suggesting a larger than life occurrence where he gains a clear insight into what needs to be done.

You should expect to be struck with similar emotions. The power of the experience is what gives you the certainty about the path you're taking. Of course, you may not hear the voice of Jesus, but this does not make your Eureka moment any less valid. You definitely shouldn't make the mistake of thinking your lack of religious faith will exclude you from this experience. King was given his answer through the voice of Jesus, precisely because he believed in God. Therefore, it wasn't conceivable that he'd receive his Eureka moment in any other form.

Obviously, if you don't believe in God then your Eureka moment will be revealed in a different manner. It might be a sudden impulse or a vision that flashes through your mind. The form is irrelevant but there is, perhaps, one pre-requisite to experiencing such a moment – you must *believe* there's a path even when you can't see it.

King's decision to pray in his time of need demonstrated his belief in a way out of his predicament. He had an idea he might gain his answer through prayer and his faith was realised when the voice of Jesus responded.

Such a response contains an important message for you. It demonstrates that, even if you don't know what you want to do with your life at present, and are crying out for your own "just cause," you must have faith that one exists. Even if evidence is scarce, you must have the foresight to see beyond your present environment. Only this kind of belief will make a direction when all paths seem blocked and reveal the hidden opportunity that those without "faith" will never see.

The Road Less Travelled

Finding the path to greatness can be difficult at times. You may find yourself on your own and painfully aware that The System's path, which so many use for direction, is unable to help.

Martin Luther King knew exactly how this felt. When questioning his path, he describes himself as having reached the "*saturation point*," feeling weak and being unable to face his journey alone. He is a man on the point of desperation. His dream appears crushed and all of the good work he has done may amount to nothing. However, as unappealing as this experience may seem, it was something he *had* to face in order to access a deeper form of guidance.

Alone in his kitchen, at midnight, King's experience could best be described as a "soul search" - a moment when a person's whole being and purpose comes into question. For King to get direction on such an important journey, he had to go through this probing self-reflection. The layers of ego and greed had to be stripped away until all that was left was the pureness of what he wanted to achieve.

Such a process can only happen under the intense pressure created when your plans are thrown into disarray. The confusion this stirs up creates a vortex that enables you to exit the day to day reality of your struggles and capture the bigger picture of what your life *should* be about. When you can blast down to this level and glimpse the magnificence of what you are here to achieve, you have a guidance giving moment that can be returned to, and relied upon, for many years to come.

To compare yourself with King and his "soul search" might seem unrealistic but if you have dreams of greatness then you'll have to share in the struggles the greats face. Like King, you may have moments when you question the validity of your path and even your sanity. However, you shouldn't be apprehensive about the prospect of such an experience. Instead, it should be embraced.

It's only when your entire future, or even your life, is on the line that you are forced to call upon hidden resources. It may seem ironic but *your desperation demands a miracle.* Nothing else will do and it's at this point you're actually closest to your source of guidance. As a result, an answer may be revealed when, only moments before, you felt all was lost.

This is why you should not allow the prospect of a "soul search" to deter you from pursuing the path to greatness. You should also remember that The System's alternative has its own shortcomings. It may offer you the path to a reasonable amount of wealth and a quiet, danger free existence, but you'll never experience a higher level of living.

This prize is reserved for those who are brave enough to heed their calling. Their reward is an opportunity to make a genuine difference to the world. Martin Luther King knew this, and although he faced death threats and physical violence, he also got to experience the joy that comes from positively influencing people's lives.

With this in mind, your options are now clear;

Stick to The System's path and never have to face any tough, soul searching moments but forever close yourself off to greatness.

Or,

Take the road less travelled, be prepared to face all of your demons but remember that if you make it through to the other side, in the words of Martin Luther King, you'll be, "*Ready to face anything.*"

Chapter 4
The Power of Having a Dream and How to Create One

Those locked into The System's way of thinking would dismiss the idea that following your inspiration can be a valid guide to finding a path through life. They see dreams of greatness as nothing more than childish fantasies. Furthermore, building a future upon mere feelings and instincts is a recipe for disaster. What happened to making decisions based upon reason and logic? And doesn't the inescapable need for money prevent us from taking off on some fanciful adventure?

Of course, these are valid questions but the person who dismisses the guidance-giving role that following their inspiration provides, overlooks a very important point. Inspiration creates purpose. If a person enjoys their work and is genuinely stimulated by their life, then they know exactly what they're living for. They need no elaborate explanation about how important their role is to society or how they *have* to live the way they do in order to meet the demands of modern life. For them, The System's justifications are irrelevant. They live the way they do because it makes them feel alive. They'll never wake up one day, aged 50, 60 or 70 and suddenly wonder where their life went. Instead, they know their life has meaning because they spend their days doing something they love.

This is why, ironically, your feelings can act as such a reliable guide to finding a path. They cut through The System's notions of duty, expectation and acceptability and get right to the core of what fascinates you. The sense of purpose this creates can't be underestimated. It might one day connect you with a dream that becomes the foundation of your life.

The Dream

I have a dream that one day on the red hills of Georgia the sons of former slaves and the sons of former slave owners will be able to sit down together at the table of brotherhood.
- Martin Luther King

No matter how grand or simple a dream may be, it serves the same purpose. *A dream provides focus.* Having a vision for your life steadies your ship when facing the challenges of escaping The System. Whether you keep it locked in your subconscious or written down on paper, your dream gives guidance through the foundation it provides.

Martin Luther King knew this well. He built his movement on a dream. By giving his followers a vision of a better life, he kept them motivated while enduring the hardships of racism, imprisonment and violence. Their day to day realities may have been bleak, but the dream they cherished in their mind was golden. By focusing on this, their thoughts were fixed on where they wanted to be, preventing a loss of morale that would have been fatal to the cause.

Your task is to create a similar guidance giving dream. When doing so, it's important not to rely on The System's obsession with consumption. Your dream has to be something more than the hope of being relatively rich, going on two holidays a year and living in a large house. While these achievements might boost your ego, they are not going to motivate you enough to break free from The System. For this, something else is required.

The perfect guidance giving dream connects with what you feel is your purpose. It has to be deeper than the desire for material success alone. You have to dream of creating a *legacy*, whether small or large, that makes a difference to yours and other people's lives. Only a dream with this kind of power will provide a focus you can return to day in day out.

Creating such a meaningful dream may be difficult. How many of us are aware of our life's purpose? Even the most driven and successful might not have a clue. For this reason, you have to start small. You are not expected to have the next five years of your life mapped out. Instead, it's enough to simply have inklings and ideas. Using these as a guide, you can begin to piece together a vision for your life that inspires.

Of course, material success may be a part of that dream and this is perfectly normal. However, to really dig out the deeper emotions of your soul, this dream must also include some genuinely life enriching qualities.

- The pursuit of perfection in everything you do.
- The thought of your work contributing to humanity's advance.
- The thought of being free to live your life exactly as you choose.
- The warmth of spending lots of time with people you love.

You have to dig deep. Think of the dramatic climax to your favourite film or book. Remember the ecstasy of your favourite sports star lifting the championship trophy. Look back into your own past successes. Use any motivating experience you can find to create your own moment of triumph. The only criteria is to get the goose bumps going.

Once you've created your dream, you can either replay it in your mind or commit to paper. Either approach will work so long as you return to this dream on a frequent basis. Subconscious programming is the key. You want to dwell on your dream to such an extent it can produce feelings of motivation and drive with each recollection.

A note of caution must also be struck though. It's important to realise that creating a dream doesn't immediately change your reality to match the likeness of your vision. It may be many years before you can say you've realised it. During this time, you might have moments when your dream seems so out of harmony with your present reality that your chances of success appear laughable.

To some, these moments are indicators that dreams create false hope. You'll have to take a different view. You'll have to understand it's in these moments that a dream is at its most valuable. It's when you believe a greater life is beyond your reach you most need the inspiration a powerful dream can provide. Without this boost, it's all too easy to interpret every failure as evidence you're doomed to a life of mediocrity. Remember, though, with a purpose, daily difficulties are put into perspective.

Now you've been introduced to the necessity of having a dream, it's time to further explore how this vision can help. The next two examples demonstrate how it can literally save your life and provide direction even when you only have a vague idea of where you want to go.

A Life Saving Dream

A dream can sustain you even when your life is at risk. The following example demonstrates this power by giving you an insight into one man's life saving dream. It's taken from Joseph Murphy's book, *The Amazing Laws of Cosmic Mind Power,* and recalls the story of a Colonel who was captured as a prisoner during the Korean War.

Lieutenant Colonel I.P. Carne told of his life as a prisoner in Korea. During his eighteen months in solitary confinement, he did not have a bitter word for the actions of his captors in imposing a sentence so harsh that doctors were amazed at his survival. In his imagination he walked around his garden (in England), and listened to the church bells welcoming him home. Lieutenant Colonel Carne said, "The mental picture of this glorious place (his loved ones, his garden, his home) forever kept my mind alive. Not for one moment did I let it slip away."

Instead of resenting or hating or indulging in mental recriminations, he gave himself a constructive vision. He imagined himself home with his loved ones; he felt the thrill and joy of it all. Visualising the garden in full bloom, he saw the plants grow and bring forth fruit. It was vivid and real in his mind. He felt all this inwardly in his imagination. He said other men would have gone insane or perhaps would have died of a broken heart, but he saved himself because of a vision. "It was a vision I never let slip away."

Lieutenant Colonel Carne's great secret was a new mental attitude in the midst of privation, misery and squalor. He was loyal to his mental picture, and he never deviated from it by destructive inner talking or negative mental imagery. Finally, when he arrived home in England, he realised the significance of the profound truth that we go where our vision is.[9]

This story is miraculous because it suggests the Colonel was sustained by his mind alone. His dream, and the subsequent positive state it created, was strong enough to shield him from the depravation of a POW camp. He experienced starvation, appalling living conditions and long hours of isolation, yet this still didn't affect his mental wellbeing. Such amazing resilience demonstrates just how important having a dream (and holding onto it) can be.

Clearly, any person seeking a greater life would be keen to tap into this power. However, the Colonel's vision was no ordinary dream and for yours to have a similar impact, you must follow his example.

The key point is that the Colonel's dream was beyond a hope or wish he'd one day return home to see his family. Instead, *it was a part of his being.* The Colonel hints at this when he mentions, "*It was a vision I never let slip away.*" Added to this, we hear how he felt the thrill and joy of his dream and even though trapped in a POW camp, the thought of being at home was, "*vivid and real in his mind.*" With such language, the Colonel demonstrates it's not enough to simply create a dream. Instead, you have to *live in its reality.*

To do this, you must experience the thrill of having achieved your dream even without taking the steps necessary for its accomplishment. This means that no matter the circumstances, you are able to live as if you are in the place you long to be. For example, if your dream is to create a successful health and fitness blog or YouTube channel then you imagine yourself gaining your one hundred thousandth subscriber and feeling the satisfaction of people all over the world contacting you to say how you've improved their lives. If your dream is to run your own martial arts studio then you see a room packed full of students and feel the excitement of them competing and winning tournaments. If your dream is to be a successful political campaigner then you imagine a new law being passed and feel the satisfaction of helping people who once suffered. Take the energy the outcome would provide and live with it NOW.

Living in the reality of your dream might be difficult at first. There may be little in your present environment that gives reason to rejoice and even less evidence your dreams can be achieved. For some, this makes living in the reality of their dream an unrealistic demand. Life is not a bed of roses so how can you pretend that it is? Given the difficulties you may currently experience, this attitude is completely understandable. However, *so much rests on developing an ability to transcend your suffering.* You need to be dynamic to forge a path to greatness.

Nothing made this clearer to me than watching, *Unforgiveable Blackness*, a documentary on the first ever black heavyweight boxing champion of the world, Jack Johnson. His was an audacious dream. In a system where black and white were forbidden to fight, he imagined himself claiming the sports ultimate prize. To do this, he spent years chasing down the white champion and opening closed door after closed door. Everybody told him it wasn't possible (not defeating Tommy Burns, just getting him in the ring to fight!) but he finally made history in 1908 when he claimed the championship.

In the documentary, various luminaries comment on Johnson's impact. The most profound comes right at the end when writer, Stanley Crouch, talks about Johnson and what it takes for a person to realise their dream:

> He's the kind of person who could have only come about in the United States. Because America, for

whatever its problems, still has a certain kind of elasticity, a certain kind of lassitude, that allows the person to dream a big enough dream that can be achieved if the person is as big as the dream.[10]

Who *you* need to become to realise your dream is something you must be aware of as you walk your path. Someone who is always down about their predicament, and frequently dwells on the possibility of failure, is unequipped to succeed. They won't have the charisma needed to convince anyone to follow them. They won't have the drive to keep bouncing back after defeat. And they won't have the creativity needed to come up with innovative ideas that capture customers attention. All of these qualities are vital, and amazingly, can be accessed regardless of your present situation.

Divine Purpose

When creating your dream, you might be surprised to learn it doesn't have to be a detailed masterpiece. In fact, as the next example demonstrates, it can be relatively vague yet still keep you on track.

Bruce Wilkinson is a pastor who claims a small prayer, hidden in an obscure part of the Bible, transformed his life. He was so convinced by the power of this prayer he wrote a book about its use.

This book became the bestselling *Prayer of Jabez* in which Wilkinson recalls the tale of the biblical character of this name. However, it's not much of a story as Jabez is only given a few lines of the bible in the frequently overlooked Chronicles section.

All that we learn of him is that he suffered and needed help. His remedy to this situation was to make a prayer to God. This prayer was answered and we hear nothing more.

As vague as the tale of Jabez may be, though, Wilkinson's discovery of it changed his life. At the time, he was a theology student, unsure about what to do when his studies finished. To assist him, a teacher pointed him in the direction of the prayer of Jabez and he started to repeat it on a daily basis. Soon his life, like Jabez's, became filled with blessings and he was propelled into a successful career as a pastor, campaign worker and author.

With such a transformation, you might expect this prayer to be a miracle making masterpiece, but it turns out to be rather nondescript. Wilkinson simply uttered the following words, *"Oh, that you would bless me indeed, and enlarge my territory, that your hand would be with me, and that You would keep me from evil, that I may not cause pain!"*[11]

At first glance there seems to be nothing special about these lines. All they ask for is a blessing, the enlarging of territory and God's protection. There is no mention of exactly how this is going to happen or with what quantity of money. Instead, it's just a vague request for an improved life. However, as vague as it may be, it still contains power.

This power is found in Wilkinson's *desire* for a better life. Although he didn't have a dream in the sense that the Colonel did, he was always thinking about a greater future. In the end, his *persistent focus on what he wanted* guided him to a greater life.

Interestingly, he didn't have to force this process. He simply repeated the words and after a while his mind was guided towards the opportunities, information and knowledge that helped him realise those deeply held desires. Like tuning a radio to a certain frequency, it wasn't possible for him to pick up any other stations while his mind was fixed on one specific outcome.

This transformation may appear to be a miracle but Wilkinson reveals the power behind the prayer later in the book. He explains that, "*His kindness in recording Jabez's story in the Bible is proof that it's not who you are, or what your parents decided for you, or what you are 'fated' to be that counts. What counts is knowing who you want to be and asking for it.*"

From these comments, it seems simply *desiring* a greater life is enough to find a path. As Wilkinson says, it's about "*knowing who you want to be and asking for it.*" He wanted to be wealthier and live a blessed life. These are qualities most people desire. However, the distinction between Wilkinson and most people is, that through the constant repetition of his prayer, he was *alive* to this idea.

This difference in focus alerts us to a subtle but fundamental distinction. A lot of people want to live greater lives but there's no belief or real expectation behind their wishes. They may occasionally fantasise about being famous or winning the lottery but that's as far as it goes. There is no obsessive drive or continual mental preoccupation. As a result, their minds aren't fully tuned in to the possibility of greatness.

With a prayer or a dream, though, you achieve this level. You deliberately state your desire and because of this, it becomes an intention. When this occurs, you enter a different realm altogether. For the first time, your simple desire now becomes something you feel compelled to act on.

At this stage, this is enough. All you need to do is know you want to move in a more fulfilling, lucrative or adventurous direction and keep repeating this intention. With time, a clearer path will emerge but you must remember that *repetition* is the key. Wilkinson repeated the prayer of Jabez on a daily basis. If you can display a similar dedication, you'll be connected with a power that can reshape your life in surprising and often amazing ways.

The Power of Your Thoughts

"We become what we think about all day long," according to Ralph Waldo Emerson. "There is nothing either good or bad, but thinking makes it so," Shakespeare tells us. Abraham Lincoln said, "People are about as happy as they make up their mind to be." "Change your thoughts and you change your world" was how Norman Vincent Peale put it. Jesus tells us, "As you think, so shall ye be."

Our futures are formed by the thoughts we hold most often. We literally become what we think about, and we are all given the gift of being able to write our own story. For me this is as close to an absolute truth to anything I know.[12]

- Wayne Dyer *(You'll see it when you Believe it)*

Our thoughts are powerful. Whether we realise it or not, they play a profound role in shaping the direction of our lives. Focus on a greater life and with time you will witness the materialisation of all the people, events and circumstances necessary for the fulfilment of your dreams. Have no focus, or get side tracked by your daily struggles, and you will fall victim to forces that appear beyond your control. This is the power of your habitual thinking. It can make the difference between realising your potential, and a life spent wondering what might have been.

All of the greats, whether deliberately or not, have connected with the power of their thoughts. To emulate them, your dream must be at the *forefront of your mind*. Whether you do this by repeating a prayer like Bruce Wilkinson, or just by thinking about it 5 minutes before you go to bed, doesn't matter. What counts is giving mental attention to what you want to achieve.

This is the path to greatness. An end destination fixed in your mind but no clearly defined path on how to get there. Instead, you have to forge, discover and find out what works for you. Many times, it may seem like you're walking towards a dead end but persist and you'll find a way through.

If you can stay the course then you'll discover something that offers great comfort to those who understand the role thought plays in shaping their reality. This knowledge is probably best articulated by the writer, James Allen, in his book, *As a Man Thinketh*. His message is we don't attract what we want, but what we *are*. It's only by changing our thoughts that we can change our lives. One of the most powerful passages from the book is this:

> Your circumstances may be uncongenial, but they shall not long remain so if you but perceive an ideal and strive to reach it. You cannot travel within and stand still without . . . Whatever your present environment may be, you will fall, remain, or rise with your

thoughts, your vision, your ideal. You will become as small as your controlling desire; as great as your dominant aspiration.[13]

Allen wants you to know that when directing your thoughts towards what you want to achieve, you're working with an irrefutable law. As he says, "*You cannot travel within and stand still without.*" If you take the time and effort to harmonize your thoughts with your vision of a greater life then you can't help but move in the right direction. **It *has* to happen.**

Following your Inspiration

Your upbringing may have provided you with little more guidance than the idea of following the next man and hoping for the best. You may have believed there's only one path - The System's path - and to deviate from this course results in disaster. However, perhaps now you understand your situation in a new light.

The System's path may offer a tried and tested route, but it also has pitfalls. The lost opportunity to be great, and the prospect of spending a lifetime conforming to a notion of who you ought to be, might make you think twice. If this is the case then you'll have to find a new form of guidance.

To locate this source, you'll have to search where most people are unlikely to look. Disguised in the midst of your feelings, intuitions and visions, it's a power that can turn the vague desire for a better life into a clear picture of a future that's guaranteed to motivate.

When thinking about this future, though, it's important

not to misunderstand the concept of following your inspiration. You shouldn't think that living this ideal means dropping everything and pursuing a half-baked dream. Your present environment does not need to act as an obstacle when moving towards a more exciting future. In fact, you can walk the path to greatness right now. You don't have to quit your job, change your friends or leave the country. This is because the journey starts within.

When you understand this distinction, an amazing change occurs. What was once mundane now has meaning. Even small chores or a boring job become part of the bigger picture. Consider these stages fundamental to your development and unpleasant situations will become bearable.

As well as not misunderstanding the nature of following your inspiration, you should also avoid worrying about whether the path your inspiration reveals is achievable. This is a mistake commonly made when taking the first steps along your new path. If you've spent your life being told reality is confined to a few narrow possibilities; it gets hard not to worry about the prospect of failure when swimming uncharted waters.

However, overcome this fear you must, because there's no quicker way to disconnect from your inspiration than by constantly questioning whether the life you wish to live is attainable. Fear and inspiration cannot coexist. One has to give and to the untrained mind, fear often runs away with our imaginations.

To prevent this from happening, *all considerations of outcome and achievability must be treated as secondary.* What's more important is the idea of allowing your inspiration to act as a guide. It may urge you to take a direction that, at present, seems unachievable but having the courage to follow this path is the only way to experience the "hidden hands" that will guide you towards greatness.

Chapter 5
Why your Beliefs Determine Everything

If thou canst believe, all things are possible to him that believeth.

- The Bible (Mark 9:23)

Learning to connect with, and follow, your inspiration can feel like an encounter with Pandora's Box. On the one hand, you have this exciting new approach which you're curious to use. On the other, when you open that box it unearths some challenging issues.

What escapes is your inspiration and once free it will encourage you to set your sights towards goals that seemed previously unachievable. This can be a great motivating force but what happens when the direction it leads you in clashes with what you've been led to believe is possible?

Unfortunately, an internal battle ensues, as your desires for a greater life fight it out with the conditioning of The System. This can be a tempestuous battle as, at every turn, The System will try to convince you that your dreams of greatness are unachievable. Much confusion and soul searching will follow until you learn to do one of two things. Either you deny your dreams and ignore your call to greatness. Or, learn to *change your beliefs* so you can live in a world without limits.

Truth vs. Belief

To assist you in this transformation you must learn the distinction between truth and belief. It's only once you've understood this difference that you'll be freed from the idea your dreams are unachievable. However, taking this step requires more than a stretch of the imagination. *It involves a complete reorganisation of the way you understand the world and your place within it.*

At present, The System may have influenced you to think of the world as a universal reality - a shared existence in which all people see, experience and understand life in the same way. In this universal reality there are certain irrefutable laws governing the way we live, the boundaries of our experience and dictate what is and is not possible. According to The System, your life is fixed to this reality. You have room for manoeuvre within its boundaries but there will always be certain dreams and goals that are beyond your reach.

Unfortunately, the acceptance of such an outlook has an

impact on how we view our own capabilities. Typically, *we begin to see ourselves as limited.* We may believe we have *some* abilities but these only permit us to operate within the confines of The System. When it comes to breaking free, we either lack the talent, or don't know how to get started.

Obviously, such an understanding of the world is going to prevent you from following your inspiration. At every turn, one of your ideas or dreams is going to clash with the boundaries of the reality you've been conditioned to believe in. "Life just doesn't work that way." "You're not one of the lucky ones with the rare talent to be great." These are just some the comments you're likely to hear from other people and the part of your mind still influenced by The System.

With little evidence to the contrary, it becomes all too easy to believe these statements. As a result, greatness appears little more than a fantasy, and the concept of following your inspiration, a far-fetched idea that clashes with the boundaries of possibility.

The Thinker/Prover Mechanism

Although it may seem impossible to challenge what appears to be *the truth* about the world you live in, there is a way around it. You can play a trick on The System that both releases you from its grasp and gives free reign to your inspiration. To do this, your understanding of the world and your role within it has to change. You'll have to realise The System's notion of the truth is *based on perception.* Furthermore, you'll have to open your mind to the idea there's no fixed universal reality.

For many, a world without The System's "truth" is a scary place. If nothing is set in stone then how does a person know their boundaries? What can they rely on to bring order to their life?

These can be troubling questions but the good news is that notions of "the truth" don't matter when it comes to escaping The System. *This quest deals with belief rather than truth* and it's important not to mistake the two as the same.

Most people don't understand this distinction and claim their beliefs *are* the truth. They'll say it's a truth they weren't born with the intelligence to create a successful business. They'll say it's a truth that poor health runs in the family and, therefore, they're destined to experience some horrible disease. And they'll say it's a truth some people are inherently evil and, therefore, we need laws and regulations to protect us. However, if you want to break free from The System then you'll have to realise your beliefs about yourself and life *do not necessarily constitute the truth*.

In fact, the best decision you could make is to remove all concepts of the truth from your mind. Once you have done this, you are free to explore the world of belief.

To understand the nature of belief it's important to realise it's not your abilities or the world you live in that determines how your life plays out. Instead, *it's your beliefs about your abilities and the world you live in that set the boundaries for your experience.*

Think about it like this; imagine you'd spent your entire life wearing a pair of red tinted sunglasses. Everything you'd see would have a red coloured tint. Would that make it "the truth" that the world is coloured with a red tint? No, but if those sunglasses were irremovable, you'd never experienced normal vision, and all the people you knew wore the same pair, you'd believe it was so.

Our beliefs are like that pair of red tinted sunglasses - a way of looking at the world. They'll filter all of the information we take in through our senses and with it, create a meaning that corresponds to our original belief. This point is further explained using a theory created by Robert Anton Wilson.

> The writer Robert Anton Wilson suggests a dual mental mechanism of the "thinker" and the "prover." He suggests that once the "thinker" has developed a belief about any aspect of existence, the "prover" will adjust the input from our senses to validate the belief. The maxim is "What the thinker thinks, the prover proves." It is the basis for our self-fulfilling prophecies.
>
> A classic story from abnormal psychology illustrates the point. A patient believes he is a corpse. He doesn't eat or work, he just sits around claiming to be a corpse. The psychiatrist tries to convince him that he is not a corpse by saying, "Do corpses bleed?"
>
> The patient thinks about that and says, "No, all body functions have shut down so they wouldn't bleed." So the psychiatrist pricks him with a needle and the man starts to bleed. The patient looks amazed, and exclaims, "I'll be damned, corpses do bleed!"
>
> Trying to talk about the existence of God to a believer is another example. People filter facts through their beliefs. It is the facts that will usually get distorted as a result, not the beliefs.[14]

Wilson's theory demonstrates how easily people can mistake their beliefs for the truth. It suggests that, through the thinker/prover mechanism, we are hard wired to validate our own beliefs. Therefore, if we have an assumption about our own ability and the way the world works, we'll subconsciously seek evidence that convinces us of the validity of this belief.

I had a lot of experience with the thinker/prover mechanism through my work as a hypnotherapist. It was never more evident than when I was trying to help those wanting to lose weight. These clients typically entered my office with a belief they were fat and unattractive. From talking to them it was clear that once they formed this belief, their subconscious set about finding evidence to validate their thoughts.

They would tell me about overhearing parts of a conversation and imagine people were discussing how fat they were. They'd go to a family reunion and interpret the looks of distant relatives as shock at how much weight they'd gained. They'd walk down the street and imagine people in passing cars were making jokes about their size. Everything they'd see or hear would reinforce the belief they had about being fat and unattractive.

Of course, most of the time, nobody was looking at them and friends and family weren't talking about how much weight they'd gained. However, because they had a negative belief about the nature of their appearance, their senses picked up on any shred of evidence to support this belief and automatically jumped to the wrong conclusion.

Take a look at your own life now and assess whether there are any areas where you've fallen into this trap.

Perhaps there's something that, at present, you believe you can't do. It might be speaking in front of an audience, approaching members of the opposite sex or concentrating for more than a short period of time. It's likely that, whatever the thing is, for as long as you can remember, you've appeared to be incapable in this field. In fact, you've had so little success with it; you've just accepted your apparent incompetence at this particular skill or activity as "the truth."

But is it "the truth?" Have you not just fallen victim to the workings of a mind hard wired to validate your beliefs?

These are the questions you must now apply to your perceived weaknesses. It's likely you have the ability to do anything, or at least excel in the areas necessary for you to escape The System and live a greater life. However, you'll not be able to do this if you understand your beliefs as *reactive* rather than *creative*.

This distinction warrants further explanation. The System teaches us to understand our beliefs as reactive. We live in the world, grow up, have certain events and experiences happen to us and as a result, gain an understanding of what the world is like and also, our abilities within that world. We *react* to these sensory experiences and form conclusions, either negative or positive. Our brains then understand these conclusions as truths because they've been validated with our own eyes and ears.

A more greatness enhancing approach, though, is to understand your beliefs as creative. This approach realises there is a *filter* through which we funnel all our sensory information. *We don't see the world as it is (nobody ever does), we see the world through the eyes of our beliefs.*

Therefore, if we believe people can't be trusted then we'll see untrustworthy people. If we believe we're terrible public speakers we'll look out on an audience and pick up on people yawning or switching off. However, it's not that the world is really full of untrustworthy people or that all members of your audience are disinterested, it's just your beliefs are filtering the information so that's all you notice.

This is why it's SO IMPORTANT to free your mind of ALL negative beliefs about yourself and the world. If you could take one message from my writing it's this - *don't believe in anything that could harm you.* Instead, only believe the best about yourself and life.

Get even with The System by refusing to stop dreaming and always seeing the good in other people. Ironically, this is the ultimate act of defiance. Despite everything we hear in the news about wars, disease and the collapsing environment, you steadfastly refuse to lose your faith in your own, and humanities, ability to turn things around.

This applies on a personal level as well. No matter how difficult your present circumstances may be, you hold onto a vision of yourself as a great person fully capable of living the life you dream of. Do so and it won't be long before the Thinker/Prover mechanism begins to work in your favour. You'll notice other people willing to help, examples of your ability to succeed and all the opportunities that do exist.

Get to this level and you're working with a positivity loop that virtually guarantees success. Because your filters are picking up on all of the reasons to be confident, happy and optimistic, you're approaching your life with an energy that can't help but bring about your desired outcomes. Of course, you'll still notice the troubles of the world, and your own imperfections, but this just reminds you to strengthen your belief in all that's good.

A Checklist for Greatness

So far, I've given you a lot of theory. I'll now get to the crux of what I want to explain.

You live in a world of limitless opportunity and possess unlimited ability. YOU CAN DO ANYTHING. The life you dream of living is attainable. However, because of The System's conditioning, you unwittingly create boundaries around what you can experience and limits on your abilities.

Much like Neo in *The Matrix*, you're conditioned into accepting a false reality. And because this false reality is so prevalent (you see it on TV, hear about it from your friends, get told to follow it by your parents, read about it online and in the papers and are coerced into accepting it in your job) you begin to mistake it as *the truth*.

There's a lot of power attached to this word "truth." It means unchangeable, unchallengeable, fixed and the same today as it will be for the rest of time. I hope you're beginning to see why this is such a problem. If you look at reality The System imposes on you as *the truth* then you'll believe your present situation cannot be changed. However, if you see The System's conditioning for what it really is – just one (of many) ways of looking at the world - then you can begin to explore your potential for greatness.

We now come to the most important part in this chapter, possibly the book. The list I'm about to give you will both make sense of the previous sections and provide a reference point for your future development. My advice is to print it out or make a copy you can put in a prominent place. It's here to remind you that you're not a prisoner to the way you're told the world works. You have the potential to be free and experience everything life has to offer.

To realise this potential, though, you must undergo a change of belief. The following list will help you do this.

System beliefs you need to reject:

- Only the exceptionally talented or lucky get to live extraordinary lives.

- The individual can't make a difference.

- You can't be happy all the time.

- Dreams only come true in movies.

- The only person you can trust is yourself.

- I am too old to live my dreams.

- I am too young and inexperienced to live my dreams.

- Authority should be respected and obeyed.

- We all have our limits.

- There are some illnesses, predicaments and circumstances you can't bounce back from.

- Scientists and Doctors know all the answers and we should do everything they say.

- Life is a struggle.

- You should be proud of your country.

- My race, class, religion and nationality define me.

- No matter how hard you work, luck will determine most of your outcomes.

- We are limited by our upbringing and environment.

- Money makes the world go around.

- I am just another ordinary person.

Greatness facilitating beliefs you need to adopt:

- I can do anything.

- The world is full of opportunity.

- Anything is possible.

- Other people are trustworthy and willing to help.

- I have the power to determine the direction of my life.

- Everything and anything can change.

- I am always learning and getting stronger.

- Life is a miracle.

- I am destined for greatness.

- People are good.

- I am complete.

- I can be happy and have something interesting to do every single day of my life.

- I can be healthy my entire life.

- My working life can be fun and rewarding.

- We can all be rich, both financially and spiritually.

- There can be peace and understanding throughout humanity.

- There is a solution to every problem.

Are these beliefs a true reflection of your life and the world at this moment in time? No (but neither are the first set). Will they enable you to live a limitless life? Absolutely, and that's the only criteria you should judge them by.

Can you see what I'm doing here? I want you to give serious consideration to your beliefs about yourself, and life, and ask whether they help or hinder your progress. Forget

The System's model of focusing on what it tells us is "the truth" and start adopting beliefs enabling you to be great.

The Training Ground for Greatness

Luke Skywalker: *I don't believe it!*
Yoda: *That is why you fail.*
- Star Wars V: The Empire Strikes Back

Previously, you may have thought your beliefs occurred as a result of observations concerning the truth about yourself and life. You've now been introduced to the idea the relationship is reversed - *your beliefs actually shape your understanding and experience of reality.*

This change of emphasise can be hard for some to grasp. If you've been raised in a system teaching you to believe in a fixed reality, the idea a person can change their beliefs and transform their life, can be difficult to accept. Instead, you might argue your beliefs are the truth and, therefore, unalterable. However, if it is greatness you desire, the Catch-22 situation you face is that *your life won't change until you change your beliefs.*

This is the paradox anyone wishing for a greater life must overcome. Your present reality may confront you with evidence of all your failures and flaws but somehow, you'll have to deny what appears to be the truth and instead, believe in what you want to become.

This predicament could be described as the training ground for greatness. It's ground zero. You have dreams and aspirations and yet you're starting from a reality that is far from perfect. As T. S. Eliot said,

Between the idea
And the reality
Between the motion
And the act
Falls the shadow[15]

To cross the shadow, you'll need an incredible amount of self-belief and the hardest steps occur when all your failures and faults are at their most apparent. This is usually at the start of your quest when you might take stock of your life and find yourself wanting.

It's from this position that dreams of greatness appear to be at their most unachievable. You might be completely reliant on an unfulfilling job to provide you with the money necessary to survive. On top of that, you may lack the qualifications or capital to put any of your ideas into action. What's more, a lifetime of conformity has robbed you of the confidence needed to follow your own path. All of these predicaments, and more, could be confronting you at this present moment. On days when they combine to remind you of the mountain you face, your situation may appear completely overwhelming. How do you then believe you're destined for greatness when confronted with a reality that's far from great?

Such a predicament could be compared to Luke Skywalker's in the dialogue above. In this scene, taken from *The Empire Strikes Back*, he is receiving Jedi training under the watchful eye of Yoda. While learning to move objects through the The Force, Luke is distracted as his spaceship sinks into the swamp. For Luke, this is a disastrous event. The spaceship is his only means of transport off the planet.

However, for Yoda, this seemingly hopeless situation is the perfect opportunity to teach Luke about the power of belief.

What follows, is a classic example of a teacher trying to expand his pupils' consciousness by getting him to believe in something he previously thought impossible. Yoda proceeds to tell Luke to raise the spaceship out of the swamp using The Force. Luke attempts, but doesn't *really* believe this is possible. Of course, with this attitude he fails and the ship barely moves.

Yoda does believe, though, and when he uses The Force, the ship is lifted high out of the swamp and onto dry land. This feat leaves Luke stunned. He utters the line, "*I don't believe it*," to which Yoda replies, *"That is why you fail."*

This scene perfectly captures the nature of Luke's Jedi training. Yoda must turn him into a believer. To fulfil his destiny as the man who brings balance to the galaxy, Luke must face constant danger and develop abilities he never thought possible. None of this will happen if Yoda can't get him to expand his consciousness and change his belief system. Luke must learn that The Force controls what he knows as reality. Therefore, the physical world he understands as *fixed* can actually bend to his wishes, so long as he learns to believe.

Although fictional, Luke and Yoda's example still bears relevance. If you were Luke, the spaceship would represent your desire for a greater life and the swamp, your present existence. The spaceship sinking into the swamp symbolises your dreams being overwhelmed by your day to day life in The System. Then along comes Yoda (this book), telling you that you can set the spaceship free (live a greater life). However, you're so consumed by the swamp (The System) you don't believe it's possible. Even when you see Yoda raising the ship (examples of other people achieving greatness) you still refuse to accept you can do the same.

Finally, you're informed why your life has failed to take off. Your lack of belief confines you to a world where many outcomes aren't possible. With this explanation, you are given the key to setting the spaceship free. *Self-belief, no matter how desperate your situation, is an absolute necessity.* Not just for what you can do with it, but for *what you can't do without it.*

Creating New Beliefs

Just as Luke's training involved a great deal of frustration and failure, you will also experience many trials while learning to use the power of belief. It's not as simple as walking around affirming, "I am a winner, I am a winner" and expecting your life to change. The beliefs you develop have to be relevant to what you want to achieve. Ask yourself this question; what will I need to believe about myself and the world I live in to enable me to live a greater life?

It's likely the answer will reveal something different to your current set of beliefs. Perhaps you'll need to believe there's a place in the world for your unique idea or that other people will accept you for who you are. Perhaps you need a greater belief in your ability to succeed or faith in your skill to convince others of your value. Or perhaps you simply need to believe a change from your present reality is possible. Whatever it is that's going to give you the boost needed to continue moving towards a greater life, must be believed in.

Adopting these new beliefs may feel awkward. There will still be a part of you saying, "it's not me, it's not the truth, so how can I pretend and walk around believing it's so?" If this is the case, then it's important to remember that your new beliefs shouldn't be judged on whether they represent the truth but instead, *on whether they grant you the opportunity to advance.*

This is the only measure when it comes to creating new beliefs. By believing you possess whatever it takes to realise your dreams, you give yourself the opportunity to achieve them. It's not a magic formula, just simple logic. No belief in an outcome means you're switched off to it occurring. Belief in an outcome gives you infinite chances for it to occur.

After you've overcome the initial unease of getting used to your new beliefs, you'll face your next challenge. How are you going to react to failure?

While attempting to cross "the shadow" there will be many occasions when you experience setbacks. If you treat them as evidence that your new beliefs are false, and confirmation of what you initially believed about yourself and the world, then the chances of rising above your present reality are slim. However, if you understand that it takes time to become your new belief, then failure doesn't seem like such a disastrous event.

Furthermore, you may start to understand that using the power of belief is not about working instant miracles. It takes time for the magic to reveal itself. The process is systematic, must be worked on daily, and, at times, can be slow. Persist with a belief in your ability to live a greater life, though, and you'll discover that no setback can stop you from getting to where you want to go.

Belief: The Secret to Success?

Many people search for the secret to success. The System wants us to believe in a winning formula, which if discovered, will unlock a life of greater power and wealth. This can be seen with the rows of lifestyle magazines filling our shops, each promising the latest discovery that will radically alter our lives. It can be seen with the courses we're encouraged to take, each promoting the newest technique that will make us a master in our chosen field. It can also be seen with the experts we're encouraged to consult, hoping their advice is going to transform our lives or business. It's a never-ending chase for that single piece of information that will solve all of our problems and improve our lives. Ironically, we'd be a lot closer to living a greater life if we realised *this secret doesn't exist.*

If there is no secret to success, though, what can you rely on to realise your desires of breaking free from The System? Unfortunately, the answer is a lot less alluring than the promise of instant riches or techniques to boost your sales by 100%. In fact, this answer is likely to take months, if not years, to produce the kind of results some promise in a week. However, you shouldn't let this put you off because once you learn to develop a "*belief mentality,*" there will be little you can't achieve.

A "*belief mentality*" requires absolute faith in everything you do. This means that with every action you take, every decision you make and every word you speak, you believe you're moving towards a greater life. There's no room for doubt, fear or questioning your decisions. Instead, you move forwards, certain in the knowledge you'll achieve your desires.

And, as a result, you succeed in everything you do and live happily ever after. The end.

Not quite, dear reader, as I'm sure you'll discover. Sometimes you won't display perfect judgement when making decisions and words will fail you on important occasions. Fortunately, though, when developing a "belief mentality" this doesn't matter. In fact, there's only one thing you must truly understand - **success doesn't come from the particular action you take or decision you make, but an overall belief in what you're doing.**

This was something I was frequently pointing out to my tennis clients. Alongside working as a hypnotherapist, I taught a variety of ages and abilities and it often surprised me just how many clients came looking for the *secret* to playing great tennis. I would give advice on technique and tactics, but sometimes had to explain there's no one right answer when it comes to finding a means to achieving your goals.

To reinforce this point, I'd mention the story of former tennis champion, Ille Nastase. In his autobiography, *Mr Nastase*, he talks about the fact he never had a tennis lesson during his youth. Growing up in Romania, without television, little exposure to top level tennis and remaining within the Iron Curtain until he was 18, he had very little external input into his tennis game. As he says, *"I didn't have a clue; I just played instinctively, because my technique was never taught to me.*" However, he was still able to succeed, holding the number 1 ranking and winning 2 grand slam titles during his career.

This story would surprise some of my clients. They expected there to be a magic secret to playing tennis that every professional and coach must know. When they found out Nastase became a professional without ever having had a lesson, their understanding of what it took to improve altered.

At this point, I tried to explain it's not so much about discovering a secret we all must learn, but believing in your ability and seeing where this *leads*. For example, one month they might have to make an alteration to their serve to gain extra power. The next, after a losing a match to a defensive player, they would have to improve their ability to close out a point. What they needed to understand was that the keys to success were always changing. It was only if they kept believing in their ability to succeed, they could keep up with this progression and fulfil their potential.

For those still determined to find the secret to success, probably the closest you'll get is the power of belief. To use this effectively, you'll have to realise it's not about the approach you take but *a belief in what you're doing* that brings results. This is the foundation for success and once you've established this base, answers will follow.

Answers on their own, with no overall belief in the direction you're going, are only half the picture. Everything should work, but for some reason it doesn't. This is because frantically *searching* for an answer implies you lack faith in your ability. It's a mentality that says, "I don't have it, I need to find it." As a result, your focus is always centred on what you lack. However, if you have a *"belief mentality,"* your approach is different. You effectively say, "I have my answer, I know what I'm doing, let's move towards greatness."

The difference between the two approaches is subtle, but the gulf between the results they produce is vast. One leads to frustration, as you continue to search for an elusive secret, bouncing from one solution to the other but never making any gains. The other leads to success, as your belief reveals whatever you need to know to continue your advance.

This is the main benefit of adopting a "belief mentality." It's the *relaxed* approach to success. There's no worrying over whether you've made the right choice. Instead, there's a calm certainty, putting you in the perfect state to achieve your objectives.

Chapter 6

How to use the Power of Belief

Training camp starts now. Just as Luke Skywalker had to master The Force, you will now be shown how to use the power of belief. The following chapter focuses on different aspects of applying this power with the ultimate goal of assisting you in developing a "belief mentality." With this supreme self-confidence, like Luke Skywalker, you will be able to bend the material to your wishes.

The Placebo Effect

The first part of your training focuses on the lessons learned from the Placebo Effect. There are few examples that provide better evidence of the power of belief than this medical phenomenon.

A fake medication (typically with a main ingredient of water, sugar or salt) is administered to a patient in the form of a pill or injection. However, the patient is not aware that the medication has no healing properties. Instead, they take it in good faith, believing it has genuine power to heal them of their ailment.

Amazingly, this belief can bring about incredible changes. Although the patient has received an injection or pill that contains nothing more than water, sugar or salt, their belief in what they think is a scientifically proven drug can facilitate changes that heal them of their ailment.

One of the most powerful examples of the Placebo Effect can be seen with the case of Mr Wright. In this story, a man who was terminally ill with cancer (Mr Wright) is treated with mixture of useless drugs and then water. The result, reported below by Dr Philip West, reveals the extent to which the power of belief can transform an individual's life. I include the case study in full as, although long, its true power and implications cannot be fully appreciated in paraphrased form.

> Mr Wright had a generalised far advanced malignancy involving the lymph nodes, lymph sarcoma. Eventually the day came when he developed resistance to all known palliative treatments. Also, his increasing anaemia precluded any intensive efforts with x rays or nitrogen mustard, which might otherwise have been attempted. Huge tumour masses the size of oranges were in the neck, axilas, groin, chest and abdomen.

The spleen and liver were enormous. The thoracic duct was obstructed, and between 1 and 2 litres of milky fluid had to be drawn from his chest every day. He was taking oxygen by mask frequently, and our impression was that he was in a terminal state, untreatable, other than to give sedatives to ease him on his way.

In spite of all this, Mr. Wright was not without hope, even though his doctors most certainly were. The reason for this was that the new drug that he had expected to come along and save the day had already been reported in the newspapers! Its name was "Krebiozen" (subsequently shown to be a useless, inert preparation).

Then he heard in some way that our clinic was to be one of a hundred places chosen by the Medical Association for the evaluation of this treatment. We were allotted supplies of the drug sufficient for treating 12 selected cases. Mr. Wright was not considered eligible, since one stipulation was that the patient must not only be beyond the point where standard therapies could benefit, but also must have a life expectancy of at least three, and preferably six months. He certainly didn't qualify on the latter point, and to give him a prognosis of more than 2 weeks seemed to be stretching things.

However, a few days later, the drug arrived, and we began setting up our testing program which, of course, did not include Mr. Wright. When he heard we were to begin treatment with Krebiozen, his enthusiasm knew no bounds, and as much as we tried to dissuade him, he begged so hard for his "golden opportunity," that against my better judgment, and against the rules of the Krebiozen committee, I decided I would have to include him. Injections were to be given three times weekly, and I remember he received his first one on a Friday. I didn't see him again until Monday and thought as I came to the hospital he might be moribund or dead by that time, and his supply of the drug could then be transferred to another case.

What a surprise was in store for me! I had left him febrile, gasping for air, completely bedridden. Now, here he was, walking around the ward, chatting happily with the nurses, and spreading his message of good cheer to any who would listen. Immediately I hastened to see the others who had received their first injection at the same time. No change, or change for the worse was noted. Only in Mr Wright was there brilliant improvement. The tumour masses had melted like snowballs on a hot stove, and in only these few days, they were half their original size!

This is, of course, far more rapid regression than the most radio-sensitive tumour could display under heavy X-Ray given every day. And we already knew his tumour was no longer sensitive to irradiation. Also, he had no other treatment outside of the single useless "shot."

This phenomenon demanded an explanation, but not only that, it almost insisted that we open our minds to learn, rather than try to explain. So, the injections were given three times weekly as planned, much to the joy of the patient, but much to our bewilderment. Within 10 days [Mr Wright] was able to be discharged from his "death – bed," practically all signs of his disease having vanished in this short time. Incredible as it sounds, the "terminal" patient, gasping his last breath through an oxygen mask, was now not only breathing normally, and fully active, he took off in his plane and flew at 12,000 feet with no discomfort!

This unbelievable situation occurred at the beginning of the "Krebiozen" evaluation, but within two months, conflicting reports began to appear in the news, all of the testing clinics reporting no results. At the same time, the originators of the treatment were still blindly contradicting the discouraging facts that were beginning to emerge.

This disturbed our Mr Wright considerably as the weeks wore on. Although he had no special training, he was, at times, reasonably logical and scientific in his thinking. He began to lose faith in his last hope which so far had been lifesaving and left nothing to be desired. As the reported results became increasingly dismal, his faith waned, and after two months of practically perfect health he relapsed to his original state, and became very gloomy and miserable. But here I saw the opportunity to double check the drug and maybe, too, find out how the quacks can accomplish the results that they claim (and many of their claims are well substantiated). Knowing something of my patient's innate optimism by this time, I deliberately took advantage of him. This was for purely scientific reasons, in order to perform the perfect control experiment which could answer all of the perplexing questions he had brought up. Furthermore, this scheme could not harm him in any way, I felt sure, and there was nothing I knew anyway that could help him.

When Mr Wright had all but given up in despair with the recrudescence of his disease, in spite of the "wonder-drug" which had worked so well at first, I decided to take the chance and play the quack. So deliberately lying, I told him not to believe what he had read in the papers, the drug was really most promising after all. "What then," he asked, "what was the reason for his relapse?" "Just because the substance deteriorated on standing," I replied, "a new super refined, double strength product is due to arrive tomorrow which can more than reproduce the great benefits derived from the original injections."

The news came as a great revelation to him, and Mr Wright, as ill as he was, became his optimistic self again, eager to start over. By delaying a couple of days before the "shipment" arrived, his anticipation of salvation had reached a tremendous pitch. When I announced that the new series of injections was to begin, he was almost ecstatic and his faith was very strong.

With much fanfare, and putting on quite an act (which I deemed permissible under the circumstances), I administered the first injection of the double potent, fresh preparation consisting of fresh water and nothing more. The results of this experiment were quite unbelievable to us at the time, although we must have had some suspicion of the remotely possible outcome to have even attempted it at all.

Recovery from his second near terminal state was

even more dramatic than the first. Tumour masses melted, chest fluid vanished, he became ambulatory, and even went back to flying again. At this time, he was certainly the picture of health. The water injections were continued since they worked such wonders. He then remained symptom free for over two months. At this time the final AMA announcement appeared in the press – "nationwide tests show Krebiozen to be a worthless drug in the treatment of cancer."

Within a few days of this report, Mr Wright was re admitted to the hospital in extremis. His faith was now gone, his last hope vanished, and he succumbed in less than two days.[16]

Mr Wright's story is an astounding tale. It defies all conventional medical wisdom and demonstrates just how powerful a belief in an idea can be. Twice he went from being on his death bed to recovering completely and all because he believed the water injections he received were a wonder drug.

Such a recovery simply *shouldn't* happen. A commonly held "system belief" is that when a person is terminally ill with cancer there is only one outcome - death. Mr Wright's initial survival demonstrates just how life changing the power of belief can be. If it can raise a cancer-stricken patient from his death bed, imagine what it can do for you?

Mr Wright's example provides a great lesson on how to activate the power of belief. The all-important factor appears to be *your emotional state.* This can be seen in the example, where the words Dr West uses to describe Mr

Wright's state of anticipation reflect this importance. He says that Mr Wright "*became his optimistic self again*" when he heard about the new injections. He also describes his, "*anticipation of salvation*" and that, "*he was almost ecstatic and his faith was very strong.*"

This description should give you an idea of the conviction needed to turn a belief into reality. *You have to be absolutely convinced that what you want to happen will occur.* It's not good enough to have a casual or timid belief. Mr Wright did not approach his treatment thinking, "Well, I'll give it a try, it might work." Instead, he was certain what he was taking would heal him of his illness.

Perhaps it was a frenzied belief, bordering on blind faith, but in this situation, it was the only thing that could break through his life-threatening condition. In doing so, Mr Wright's example demonstrates the strength of feeling required to develop a "belief mentality." It's not enough to simply think about what you desire; you have to *feel* it as well. Your new beliefs will require an *intense emotional involvement* if they are going to assist you to recover from your own malady of a life spent suffering in The System.

Although Mr Wright's story has been presented as a triumph for the power of belief, there is no happy ending. To some, his demise may hint at the fact his recovery was only a temporary remission and ultimately, he couldn't overcome the cancer. This explanation would accredit his initial recovery to chance and therefore, fit in neatly with The System's logic that physical illness needs a physical cure.

There is another explanation, though, that counters this theory. This explanation accredits Mr Wright's demise to *misguided faith* rather than denying the impact of placebos and the power of belief. It was because Mr Wright placed all his faith in modern medicine, he was unable to sustain his recovery.

Evidence of this can be seen with his reaction to the news report that Krebiozen was useless in the treatment of cancer. On both occasions it prompted the return of his condition. Unfortunately, his faith in medical science was so strong he subconsciously allowed its dictates to determine his health. This worked when scientists were talking about a wonder drug with miracle healing properties. However, it wasn't so good when his last hope was rubbished as ineffective.

When this happened, he was doomed. He had such a fervent belief in medical science, he had nothing to fall back on.

Perhaps the only thing that could have saved Mr Wright was if he'd placed his faith in *the power of belief itself*. If he had understood it was his belief in the drug (and not the drug itself) that healed him, there's a good chance he'd have sustained his recovery. However, placing faith in the power of belief presents its own difficulties.

It's so much easier to externalise our beliefs. Throughout history we've always needed something to believe *in*. In the past it was God, a holy relic, a healing site, a witchdoctor or a ritual. Now it's science, medicine, or the government. These are some of the external powers through which we've channelled our beliefs. Ironically, we'll allow ourselves to believe in them but when it comes to placing faith in the force that acts through these institutions – belief itself - we falter.

Perhaps this is because, in doing so, it also means we have to believe in ourselves. When you live in a system that teaches dependence on it and its institutions, believing in yourself, against all the odds, is a step only the great will take.

In case you have not got the message, let me be absolutely clear:

1. Belief itself (as opposed to the object of belief) is the most powerful tool for change that human beings possess.
2. Most people expend their powers of belief on external things, but the great appropriate it for themselves.
3. Whatever we decide to believe about ourselves (whether "true" or not) must become our reality.

The mind/body connection

Both the case of Mr Wright, and the numerous other examples of healings through placebos, suggest a strong mind/body connection. It appears our thoughts and beliefs have a direct influence over our physical being. In the case of Mr Wright, it appears his positive emotional state set in motion a chain of physical reactions that returned him to health. His body was compelled to match the idea he had of himself as a healed man. Ironically, this mind/body connection then worked against him when he heard the report rubbishing the effects of Krebiozen. He immediately became depressed, lost all faith and, as a result, his cancer returned. Therefore, in both his healing and remission, it appears that his mind determined the health of his body.

Such a revelation has implications far beyond the realm of health. If translated to the quest for greatness, the mind/body connection indicates that an overwhelming belief in success will lead to the realisation of your desires. Just as Mr Wright's body was compelled to reflect the understanding he had of himself as a healed man, you will be motivated to search out all of the people, events and ideas in harmony with your vision of a greater life.

This makes perfect sense. If you have an unshakable belief in your ability to accomplish a goal then you'll feel more motivated to take the steps necessary for its achievement. Furthermore, you'll be relaxed, confident and excited about the realisation of your desire. As a result, you'll be free to act with clarity and purpose. You'll recognise an opportunity when it comes your way, be able to push yourself beyond the normal levels of endurance and recover from setbacks without lasting negative impact. All of this will occur because you start your quest with the premise you can achieve your desire.

Contrast this approach with someone who is uncertain about their ability to achieve their goal and it becomes evident how your beliefs create a self-fulfilling prophecy. For them, being unsure about their chances of success, and maybe even believing their desire is unachievable, they'll never wholeheartedly commit to the goal they wish to achieve. As a result, they will interpret every minor failure as evidence that it's time to quit. Furthermore, they will lack the motivation to put in the daily effort needed to achieve anything worthwhile. Why would they, when they're not convinced they'd be successful even if they tried?

Such a person is cut off from the resources needed to break free from The System. This is exactly what the mind/body connection can do. Much like the thinker/prover mechanism, it operates without discrimination and can either charge you with the energy to succeed, or leave you too weak to even contemplate expanding your horizons.

The Story of Sarah: A case study on developing belief

Act as though I am, and I will be.
  - Joseph Murphy, *The Power of your Subconscious Mind*

While working as a hypnotherapist, I was occasionally aware that my results benefited from the placebo effect. Some clients would visit me with such great expectations their belief alone was enough to facilitate a change. All I had to do was match their ideal of how a hypnotherapist should be and their subconscious would do the rest.

On most occasions, though, this wasn't the case. Instead, many clients would come to the first session feeling apprehensive about what might happen. One such person was a lady called Sarah. She contacted me for help improving her confidence with public speaking and presentations. Read her story below for an insight into developing self-belief.

A promotion at work was Sarah's catalyst for booking a session. As delighted as she was to be gaining greater autonomy, creative input and money, she was secretly terrified about some of the aspects of her new role.

The prospect of pitching to major clients and speaking at conferences brought back a fear of public speaking that had been with her since school. It was during this time, she'd had a string of bad experiences speaking in front of a class. Then, the consequences had been ridicule and a few bad marks. Now, the stakes were higher. Her new role required her to speak on a semi-regular basis in high pressure situations. She simply wouldn't be able to function in this job if her performances didn't improve.

Previous to this promotion, she'd only presented to a small team in a closed environment. However, even this had caused her great anxiety and stress.

In the days leading up to these presentations, she experienced difficulty sleeping, constant thoughts of failure and became irritable at work. When it came to giving the presentation, she went into what she described as "robot mode." This involved reading sections directly from her notes and using minimal expression in her delivery. While this was sufficient for her previous role, she knew it would not be acceptable in her new position. For this, she needed to be dynamic. She was going to have to sell clients ideas and products, requiring a delivery that captivated their attention.

To achieve this transformation, we both knew significant changes needed to be made. At present, Sarah had a total lack of belief in her ability as a public speaker. She described herself as hopeless and said her performances were boring and uninspiring. However, despite these beliefs, she refused to accept it was a hopeless situation.

Pleased with this determination, I began our session by

asking some questions designed to get her thinking like a successful speaker. "How would a person who has complete faith in their speaking abilities approach presentations?" "What would they be thinking before they spoke?" "How would they stand before an audience?" "How would they project their voice while speaking?" These were some of the questions I asked as we talked in detail about what a successful speaker would think and do. I then suggested she would have to become such a person.

Although sceptical at first, Sarah understood that to become a commanding speaker, first she would have to believe in this reality. This meant seeing, feeling, hearing and understanding herself as a capable speaker before she even gave a presentation. With this is in mind, the first area we worked on were pre-presentation nerves. At present, Sarah found the days leading up to her presentations very stressful. Her mind was plagued with images of failure and embarrassment.

Obviously, this wasn't conducive to delivering a good presentation, so to lead her in the direction of what she needed to become, I asked her, "If you believed you're a confident speaker, how would you be feeling in the days preceding the presentation?" She answered that she would be calm and collected. Furthermore, there would be no worrying about the presentation because she was sure in the knowledge it would be a success.

I was delighted with this response. It was exactly the message I wanted to convey to her subconscious. So, to help it sink in, I induced trance and instructed her to embody these qualities. She had to imagine herself at work and home with a totally clear mind. We deliberately avoided thinking about the upcoming presentation (unless she was doing work preparing for it) as I wanted her to remain in the 'now'. Then, I got her to repeat an affirmation - *I am calm and confident in my abilities* - to use if she was ever struck by a moment of nervousness. Both of these instructions got her into the pre-presentation mind-set of a successful speaker.

In the next couple of sessions, we focused on her delivery. In the past, Sarah relied heavily on her notes and colleagues had described her speaking style as monotone and expressionless. She felt there was little chance of being able to convince anybody of her knowledge if she continued to deliver her presentations in this manner. So, I asked her, "If you believe you're a confident speaker, how would you deliver your presentation?" She answered, "With conviction. I would believe that every word I speak and every gesture I make penetrates the minds of the audience and convinces them of what I am saying." We then talked a bit more about how *it wasn't about what she said, but the belief behind her words* that was going to make her speaking so effective. Then, while in trance, I asked her to imagine she was in front of an audience giving a presentation. She had to believe every word she spoke was having the desired impact and convincing her colleagues and clients as if they were under her spell.

This imaginary presentation lasted about 30 minutes and took her through every stage of the process. After it was finished, she had the complete picture of herself as a dynamic speaker. Every aspect of her appearance, mannerisms, voice and impact on the audience was covered so that she had a clear blueprint to follow.

This filled Sarah with a great deal of confidence. She now felt she could measure her past thoughts, feelings and behaviour against this blueprint and correct anything that was out of line. As our sessions came to an end, she was ready to embrace the new role and use the power of belief to make an impression on her colleagues and bosses.

I next heard from Sarah two months down the line. She sent an email informing me she had done her first few presentations and they had been a success. There was still room for improvement but her pre-presentation nerves had greatly reduced and she was feeling more relaxed in front of an audience. She even received some positive feedback from clients who commented on how informative her presentations were.

Developing a Belief Mentality

For many, the idea of using the power of belief is abstract. Sports stars, business leaders and pioneers in every field may talk about how it's the secret to their success but most of us don't understand how such an intangible quality could be used to change our lives.

Fortunately, with Sarah's story, we have an example of how it can be applied. The most important point to take from her example is *you have to adopt the mentality and approach of the person you want to become.* In Sarah's case, she wanted to be a competent public speaker. Therefore, she had to develop an idea of how a competent speaker thinks, feels and presents themselves and project herself into this image.

For you, the process will be very similar. As part of your

training you must start to think, and act, like the great person you really are. Ask yourself these questions.

- Does a great person worry constantly about what might go wrong?
- How would you approach people and in what manner would you interact with them?
- How would you meet a challenge?
- What does a great person do when presented with an opportunity to advance their lives?
- What thoughts go through this person's mind? What's their emotional state on a day to day basis?

Project yourself into the person you want to be and think and act from this perspective. Of course, it takes time and the process is gradual but, ultimately, you're working with something that can't fail. Through the mind/body connection, you'll be compelled to change.

To ensure this change happens as rapidly as possible, I now offer three belief building techniques for you to master. Set up a daily routine where you incorporate one, or all, of them to develop belief in your ability to live a greater life. As an interesting aside, Tim Ferriss of *Four Hour Work Week* fame, estimates that eighty percent of guests on his podcast, which focuses on deconstructing the world's greatest performers in a variety of fields from trading to fitness, all have some kind of meditational or mind focusing daily routine.[17] Such a large proportion of peak performers can't be wrong. There's power in focusing your mind on what you want to achieve. Here's how to use yours.

Techniques for Change

Self-Hypnosis

I first came across self-hypnosis while training to become a hypnotherapist and have been using it ever since to help both my clients and myself. The best results are achieved by quietening your mind and feeding it with images and thoughts of what you want to achieve. Repeated often enough (and with enough passion) they will sink into your subconscious and be accepted as real.

This occurs because your subconscious can't tell the difference between an imagined and a real experience (it's why you suddenly wake in a state of shock after having a vivid dream or are captivated by the images you see on a movie screen). Although nothing 'real' is happening, due to your conscious mind being all but silenced, you believe in whatever is occurring. As a result, you have the perfect means for bypassing that critical "system voice" that typically forbids us from thinking anything great about ourselves. All you have to do is slow down your conscious mind (using the instructions below) and your subconscious will begin to accept the thoughts you feed it.

To benefit from self-hypnosis, your program should be tailored to your needs. You have to use the images and thoughts that push *your* buttons. Try to work with just a few. For example, if you want to create a successful blog with one hundred thousand subscribers then see that figure clearly in your mind. If you're looking for love then imagine you and your soulmate holding hands. If you want to get in shape then imagine yourself looking great or see a certain weight on the scales.

Notice how all of these images are very simple. You don't have to create an elaborate story in your mind. Just follow these brief instructions and open yourself to the experience.

- Find a place where you won't be disturbed and can comfortably relax for 10 to 15 minutes.

- Fix your eyes on an object you can see in front of you and slightly higher than your line of sight. Wait until you begin to feel your mind and body slowing down and then close your eyes.

- Start feeding your subconscious with thoughts of what you want to achieve. This has to be deliberate. It won't happen automatically, and your mind will most certainly wander at the start, but keep returning your thoughts to the thing you want to achieve. However, don't force your concentration – this will activate your conscious mind. It should be relaxed. Notice your breathing if it helps and keep gently focusing your thoughts. Use images or repeat phrases over to yourself. It doesn't matter what they are, as long as a) it's something you want to achieve/become and b) it's simple and easy to focus on.

- An emotional reaction of feeling uplifted, joyous, excited or pumped is an ideal response but not always (especially when you first start) achievable. If you do find yourself feeling this way then it means your sub-conscious is accepting what you are offering it. However, don't get frustrated if this fails to occur. Often it takes time to build up the connection. Rest assured, though, if you practise enough then you'll get to the point where your thoughts will stir deep emotions in your soul.

- Continue for as long as you feel comfortable, opening your eyes whenever you feel ready.

The power of this practise develops with repetition. Don't expect to feel like Superman after your first 10 minutes of self-hypnosis. More so, don't expect your reality to instantly change and match the likeness of your dream. It doesn't work that way. However, with practise, and time, you'll have a guaranteed method of creating a new belief.

Combine this with a few "real life" victories (which will now serve as confirmation of "the truth" of your new beliefs), and it will become almost impossible to convince you of anything other than the fact you're destined for greatness.

Written Statement

The second technique used to activate the power of belief is a written statement. This involves writing a brief passage about what you wish to occur as if it has already happened. For example, a person with an illness will write about how they *are* healed and how their body functions perfectly even if they are bed ridden. An aspiring entrepreneur will write about their huge profits and the people that enjoy their products even without having made a single sale. An up and coming sportsperson will write about lifting the championship trophy and gaining the number one ranking even before winning their first major competition.

Once created, you then repeat your statement on a daily basis, reading it over and over until its words sink into your subconscious. As with self-hypnosis, after a while, the statement will become a part of your being. You'll start believing you are that healthy, dynamic person with an exciting life even if your present reality reflects something else.

Before creating your own written statement, read the following example. It's written for a young man with aspirations of playing pro tennis.

I am a brilliant tennis player. When on the tennis court I am a master. My shots flow and I have the killer instinct that enables me to finish off a point. From the start of a match I'm focused on my goal of winning. I appear light, fast and full of energy. My serve is struck with a power that is unreturnable. My forehand and backhand always find their mark. My volleys are crisp and I put away every smash.

I walk onto the tennis court in the right frame of mind. Whether I'm practising or competing, I remain 100% focused and ready to do whatever necessary to improve and win. I feel the excitement of competition and am always able to play to the best of my abilities. Irrespective of the score, I remain calm and focused. Even in the closest of matches I am still composed and able to find that inner calm that is crucial to victory.

I am a champion. I win tournaments and experience the high of having achieved my goals.

Hopefully this example will give you some ideas. A few paragraphs are all that's necessary. Make it punchy and sharp, something that, after reading for a while, you can commit to memory. Make it descriptive too; really get your creative juices flowing. So, if it's having the wealth to enjoy financial freedom then write about the crisp feel of the cash in your hands, the excitement of being able to do what you want when you want to do it and the peace of mind that comes with knowing you'll never be trapped in a job you don't enjoy.

Above all else, though, it must be bold. There's no room for, "I hope" "I'll try" or "I wish." This is The System's timid approach to realising your desires. It's filled with notions of not asking for too much and being realistic about what you can achieve. It's too scared to challenge perceived limitations and, therefore, never gets to the core of what you desire.

To do this, you have to be brave. You have to be bold enough to say, "This is how my life is *going* to be." In fact, the whole statement has to be written as if you have already achieved whatever it is you desire. Whether it's making a certain amount of money, finding your ideal partner or discovering your life's calling, you must write it and repeat it with the utmost belief it will occur.

So, take whatever it is you desire and write your state-ment *now*. Don't get confused if you can't define your life's purpose. Just think of an area you want to improve, be it romantic, financial or personal and make a start. Of course, you can write more than one but I would recommend focusing on a specific area for a long enough period of time to realise your objective. Then, you can move onto another.

Repeat the statement three times in a row at least once a day. And for goodness sake, say it with *passion*. Get fired up about what you want. Think of yourself as a preacher or a politician addressing a huge crowd and having to convince them of your words. Make it a performance, complete with movement and actions.

As with the self-hypnosis, don't expect too much the first few times. The power of the written statement grows with repetition. When you're well versed in its recital, and can feel the meaning behind each word, then you'll be sending your statement out to the universe. **It will respond!**

And for those of you who are really stuck, and want a generic statement about living a free and great life, then feel free to use the one below.

My life is amazing. Every day I spend my time engaged in activities that stimulate my mind to the fullest. I wake up happy, refreshed and full of life. I have all the money I need. I am surrounded by beauty and feel totally at home with my environment. I have the freedom to go where I please and do what I want.

I am surrounded by people I love. My soulmate is with me and the love we share makes every day feel like a dream. I see my friends and family whenever I want. I get to work with them, hang out and have fun together. The sense of inspiration and unity that comes from having this group fills me with energy.

I am living my life's purpose. I always find solutions to

the problem I face and I know I'm having a positive impact on the world.

Prayers and Wishes

Using prayer as a means to achieving your dreams has already been covered with Bruce Wilkinson's *Prayer of Jabez*. In a nutshell, create a small ritual where certain words are spoken relating to a desire you wish to achieve. You may make this prayer to the God of your faith, the life force, universal intelligence or a God entirely of your imagination. The object of your prayer is not important, the repetition, ritual and feeling behind what you ask for is.

Don't feel guilty about praying for yourself. Of course, you may want to pray for others and you should be commended for caring, but don't let The System make you feel guilty about your own desires. You being happy, healthy and free is the best way to serve the world.

Wishes are similar to prayers. They are a desire for greatness in a particular, or all, areas of your life. They are usually connected to some routine like wishing on a coin as it's thrown into a fountain or speaking your desire to the universe as the Sun sets.

The example below will give you some idea of how to create a wishing routine. Taken from Michael Jackson's autobiography, *Moonwalk*, it focuses on the wishing rituals Jackson used to supercharge his subconscious with the belief he could create the greatest selling album of all time.

Off the Wall had sold almost six million copies in this country, but I wanted to make an album that would be even bigger. Ever since I was a little boy, I had dreamed of creating the biggest selling record of all time. I remember going swimming as a child and making a wish before I jumped into the pool. Remember, I grew up knowing the industry, understanding goals, and being told what was and was not possible. I wanted to do something special. I'd stretch my arms out, as if I were sending my thoughts right up into space. I'd make my wish, then I'd dive into the water. I'd say to myself, "This is my dream. This is my wish," every time before I'd dive into the water.

I believe in wishes and in a person's ability to make a wish come true. I really do. Whenever I saw a sunset, I would quietly make my secret wish right before the sun tucked under the western horizon and disappeared. It would seem as if the sun had taken my wish with it. I'd make it right before that last speck of light vanished. And a wish is more than a wish, it's a goal. It's something your conscious and subconscious can help make a reality . . .

There were times during the Thriller project when I would get emotional or upset because I couldn't get the people working with me to see what I saw. That still happens to me sometimes. Often people just don't see what I see. They have too much doubt. You can't do your best when you're doubting yourself. If you don't believe in yourself, who will? Just doing as well as you did last time is not good enough. I think of it as the "try to get what you can" mentality. It doesn't require you to stretch, to grow. I don't believe in that.

I believe we are powerful, but we don't use our minds to full capacity. Your mind is powerful enough to help you attain whatever you want. I knew what we could do with that record. We had a great team there, a lot of talent and good ideas, and I knew we could do anything. The success of Thriller transformed many of my dreams into reality. It did become the biggest selling album of all time, and that fact appeared on the cover of The Guinness Book of World Records.[18]

This example is relevant for a number of reasons. First, we get an insight into the mind-set that helped create the greatest selling album of all time. Jackson clearly states, "a wish is more than a wish, it's a goal." Its clear part of his success was founded on this frequent ritual of making wishes. These were linked to a particular stimulus (watching the sun set and diving into water), something that heightened their power and gave them added meaning.

However, perhaps the most important point is that Jackson understands the force that lies behind a wish. It's not an empty whisper or something from a Disney film. Instead, it's a very real means of galvanising the conscious and subconscious minds.

Such an insight should give you a great deal of reassurance. All you need is a desire, some particular act to connect it with, and the determination to keep repeating it over and over again. Your mind will do the rest, attracting you to the people, ideas and opportunities that are going to make your wish come true.

Begin thinking about your wishing routine. Like Michael Jackson, it might be a connected to a sunset or it could be every time you see a landmark that is significant to you. Perhaps you'll make your wish before you fall asleep at night or upon rising first thing in the morning. Your surroundings or the significance of the place, and time, should evoke strong emotions. This helps the wish sink into your subconscious.

Your wish should be no longer than a sentence. While working as a tennis coach, I taught a family who lived in a fantastic house with a court in their garden. Every time I pulled up to their house to teach them, I would make a wish, saying, "I will live in a house like this by the time I'm 34." The exterior of the house evoked feelings of warmth and having a happy home and the beauty of the garden, a connection with nature. Because of this, my wish felt particularly potent and at age 34, I was able to buy a flat (albeit on a much smaller scale), on a development with 21 acres of beautiful wooded land.

As well as shedding light on the effectiveness of wishes, Jackson's example also reinforces the importance of the power of belief. His key statement is, "*You can't do your best when you're doubting yourself. If you don't believe in yourself, who will?*" From these lines it's clear he knows how important it is to approach the tasks you undertake with the utmost belief in your success. Combined with his wishing rituals, he seems to have reached a level of certainty in his belief. As he says in the example, "*I knew what we could do with that record . . .I knew we could do anything.*"

This is a place any person wanting to achieve greatness should be. Such certainty is essential when overcoming the doubts and ridicule that other people routinely throw at those who desire a life above the ordinary. You might be confronted with bank managers who doubt your business plan, doctors who say you'll never recover, publishing and record companies who don't see the value in what you've created and friends and family who are scared that the whole experience of chasing dreams will leave you broken. In short, expect a tidal wave of doubt from those around you.

It's at these points all of the work put into developing your self-belief shows its value. Those days spent making wishes, channelling thoughts, reading statements and saying prayers, build a strong foundation of belief that shields you from the influence of The System. Others will fall, but with your belief strengthened on a daily basis, comments from the naysayers will only drive you to higher heights.

You'll see it, when you believe it

Developing self-belief is one of the most important steps to escaping The System and achieving greatness. However, lest you should give up on the process through temporary frustration, it is important to be aware of the transitional period that ensues.

Old beliefs die hard. Evidence of their legitimacy is ever present. You need only wake in the morning and look around to see confirmation of the boundaries that exist. That 40-inch waistline is evidence you are not the slim and attractive person you want to be. That zero in your bank account reminds you you're not a millionaire. And the job you hate lets you know that you haven't found your life's calling. All of these facts are very tangible and real.

Contrast this with a mere belief that you are destined for greater things and it's no wonder that your mind can struggle to accept the new blueprint for your life. All you have to work with are thoughts, visions and images. How can these stand up against what's concrete and real?

Unfortunately, there is little answer to this question but a lot of hard work. Along the way, you'll have to recondition your mind to understand that every little failure doesn't represent evidence that your desires are unachievable. Then, with each small success you can start to build the belief that greater goals are possible.

At some point, you *will* start to win the internal battle. The surest sign this is occurring will be provided by your feelings. When you start to feel excited or inspired about your life, you can be sure your new beliefs are sinking in. Genuine optimism can't be faked and it only comes to those who *expect* great things. Reach this point and the realisation of your dreams won't be far behind.

Chapter 7
Soul Power: The Secret to your Happiness and Success

Any person can pay lip service to the power of belief. However, to genuinely embody their beliefs a person must *feel* them throughout their entire being.

This kind of fire in your emotions can't be faked and is only developed through a clear understanding of your inner world. Without this, any belief in your own greatness will appear empty. You'll be faking it, telling yourself one thing but feeling something else.

To avoid this, a shift in your approach to life, and understanding of success, must take place. You must learn to appreciate the role of the inner world in shaping the outer and discard The System's tendency to focus simply on what you can see, hear and touch.

The Master Secret of the Ages

The first part of this shift occurs through an understanding of how The System conditions us to focus on the physical. We're a symptom society. This can be seen on a macro level; treating a failing economy by pumping more money into the financial system. It can also be seen on a micro level, with an approach to personal health that views pumping drugs into our bodies as the most effective treatment for illness.

We rarely look behind what we can see and touch to the *real cause* of the events that occur in our lives. Instead, there is a never-ending focus on results and what is physically quantifiable.

- Do you have more money than the next person?
- Are you winning?
- Do you work enough hours?

We believe that success, and value, can be measured in numbers. Always looking to accumulate more, we misguidedly believe this will enhance our quality of life.

Perhaps such an overwhelming focus on the physical is understandable. After all, it's there, in front of our eyes, in our ears and real to the touch. It's the only world we know and therefore, appears to govern everything. What else could? Surely, we find ourselves trapped in The System because of the environment we were born into, the talents (or lack of) we were given and the bad luck which has subsequently come our way?

While such an explanation appears to make sense, it's one you have to shed. To escape The System you must understand *your reality is a reflection of your inner state.* It's your thoughts, feelings and beliefs that determine your environment, not the other way around. Once you have learned this great metaphysical truth, you are truly free.

I would understand if you are sceptical about the previous statement. How can something tangible like personal finances, health and current employment be determined by thoughts and feelings? After all, The System teaches us to think it's the other way around and personal experience *appears* to validate this theory.

My aim is to lead you away from this thinking. I want to initiate you in to a deeper wisdom. While the masses experience a rollercoaster ride of emotions depending on the events of their day, the greats remain unaffected. Sometimes this is through predisposition but, mainly, it's through training. They're aware of a secret that can grant every person the freedom to determine their life. They then do everything in their power to harmonise their mind with its dictates.

To assist you in your transition to becoming one of these greats, I will now share this secret with you. Taken from Joseph Murphy's book, *The Power of Your Subconscious Mind,* it reads as follows:

> In the ancient world, Hermes Trismegistus had the reputation of being the greatest, most powerful magus the world had ever known. When his tomb was opened, centuries after his passing, those who were in

touch with the wisdom of the ancients waited with great expectancy and a sense of wonder. It was said that the greatest secret of the ages would be found within the tomb. And so it was. The secret was:

As Within, So Without;
As Above, So Below.

This same truth was proclaimed by Moses, Isaiah, Jesus, Buddha, Zoroaster, Laotze, and all the illuminated seers of the ages. Whatever you feel as true subjectively [within] is expressed as conditions, experiences and events [without].[19]

Take a few moments to fully digest this passage and let the significance of the words sink in. Get excited because you now have the means to positively shape your future and realise your dreams. Through meticulous assessment and regulation of your thoughts, feelings and beliefs, you will create an inner paradise that will find its expression in your outer world.

The difficulty, though, lies in overcoming The System's conditioning as it attempts to convince you of the importance of the physical. It wants you to believe your circumstances will determine your future. Furthermore, it wants you to see the physical world as a vast, all powerful realm that has control over your life.

You will have to deny this conditioning on a daily basis. As awkward as it may seem, you have to reach the point where you can look upon the physical world as a *reaction* to a much greater power. The government, the media, the legal system, those towering skyscrapers you see in the city, the place you work and the schools and universities where you received your education, all a *reaction* to the inner world of billions of people throughout history.

Making this shift frees you to focus exclusively on where real power lies. If you're not intimidated by the apparent dominance of the physical world, or preoccupied by the events of your life, then you can focus on your inner world. Here, you will find all you need to radically change your environment. In fact, it's easy. **Channel your thoughts towards success, alter your beliefs so anything is possible and raise your energy so that you feel great.** The "As Within, So Without" principle will do the rest.

Developing Soul Power

Soul Power is a term I use to describe an uplifting feeling that will change your life. It's the joy of being alive, the buzz of knowing you're onto something great and the excitement of performing to the best of your ability. Most importantly, developing this state is the most effective way of using the "As Within, So Without" principle.

The best way to explain Soul Power is to look at the teachings of Obi Wan Kenobi and Yoda. In the *Star Wars* trilogy, they talk about The Force - an intangible energy running through all living beings. *"Luminous beings are we,"* Yoda tells Luke, *"Not this crude matter."* He wants Luke to understand the energy that animates us (and the universe) is where he should be focusing his attention. Master it by eliminating all anger, fear and hate, and the physical world will respond to his wishes.

Soul Power is very similar to The Force. It's an energy you harness by feeling great. Like The Force it takes skill and persistence to master. Daily, you must be mindful of your feelings and make sure your energy levels remain high.

However, just as The Force could only be mastered by a select few, Soul Power is also an exclusive energy. It's impossible to use when you struggle or force through your desires. This is The System's approach to success and much like "The Dark Side" it will eat away at your soul. Instead, you must detach your mind from the physical world and focus on getting in as inspired a state as possible.

The key to doing this is *living in the state of your realised desire*. This means live as if your life is already complete. Imagine you had everything you want from this world - love, money, a passion to pursue and happiness. How would you feel? Overwhelmed, joyous, ecstatic? It's likely you would experience all these emotions and more. What I'm asking you to do is capture that feeling and then live with it on a daily basis.

Sounds easy, right? It's not. There are 101 different factors that can knock your energy. You have an argument with your boyfriend or girlfriend, your boss tells you they want you to stay late and finish up a project, someone in your family has a serious illness or the latest blog post you update to your website bombs. What happens then? I think you can guess. That nonsense about living in the state of your realised desire goes out the window as you're consumed by the negative energy of the event.

The likelihood of this occurring makes it essential to have a framework for developing your Soul Power. I suggest you follow this 5-point plan to make sure you remain inspired no matter what is going on.

1. Whenever you have any down time (i.e. travelling to and from work, taking a shower, doing household chores etc.) focus on your energy.

2. Start to build it by remembering the occasions when you felt most inspired in your life. The events, although relevant, are not as important as how you were feeling. Or, if you're short on past inspiration, then think about the life you want to create. What's inspiring you about this life? Focus on the feelings living it will generate.

3. Keep recalling the feeling. Don't worry if it feels like hard work, this is a good sign. It means a connection between your mind and spirit is being built. Continual repetition is the key. After a while, the connection will be strong enough to trigger an emotional reaction as soon as you begin to focus.

4. To boost your Soul Power even more, anchor the feeling with a physical movement. This could be clenching your fists, raising your hands towards the sky, bouncing on the spot, holding your hands in a praying position or anything else that you find relevant. Perform this action while you focus on building your energy. With time, you'll find the two complement each other and the action alone gets your Soul Power firing.

5. Repeat as often as possible and at a minimum, once a day.

Understandably, you may be a little sceptical about the concept of Soul Power. Effectively, you are being asked to *feel* your way to greatness. It probably contradicts everything you've been taught and you may still hold onto the belief that success rests on action, effort and the forcing through of your desires.

The next two examples should help remove some of the doubt. They focus on two greats, both of whom built their Soul Power by living in the state of their realised desire. Some might call them arrogant, but it was this ability to live with a dynamic energy *without* proof of their greatness, that enabled them to scale the heights in their respective fields.

Soul Power was evident in everything Muhammad Ali did. His amazing self-belief, his super confident pre-fight predictions and his flamboyant personality were all indicators of a man who was full of life. However, perhaps the greatest example of his Soul Power was the moniker he used to describe himself – "The Greatest of All Time."

Amazingly, it was a nickname he gave himself *before* he'd won a championship belt. Whereas most fighters would be struggling to establish themselves at this stage in their career, Ali already *believed he was complete.* His future career, as a three-time heavyweight champion of the world and victor in some of the most memorable fights of the 20th century, validated what, at the time, seemed to be an empty statement.

How was this success possible? Partly because of his Soul Power. The energy he generated by believing he was "The Greatest" will have removed the anxiety often associated with achievement. There was no period of questioning or self-doubt with Ali and no wasted energy worrying about whether he could make it. Instead, he lived as if he was already a champion and as a result, *his material world changed to reflect his inner state.* What many would have called imagination, soon became reality.

Arnold Schwarzenegger is another example of a great who was able to use Soul Power to realise his dreams. In his book, *The Education of a Bodybuilder,* he says, "*I knew I was a winner back in the late sixties. I knew I was destined for great things. People will say that kind of thinking is totally immodest. I agree. Modesty is not a word that applies to me in any way – I hope it never will.*"

Interestingly, this comment refers to a time *before* Schwarzenegger was officially recognised as a champion (he didn't win his first Mr Olympia title until 1970). At the time, few people outside the bodybuilding world had heard of him and he certainly wasn't the movie star, and politician, people recognise today. However, he's still talking as if he *was*, and this is the key.

Schwarzenegger's comments capture the essence of what it means to live in the state of your realised desire. It's not arrogance. It's simply a deeper understanding of how your inner state will manifest itself as the circumstances and events of your life. From this perspective, it's actually a necessity. If you want to achieve any kind of success, the blueprint must first exist in your mind.

Soul Power is the missing piece of the puzzle when it comes to escaping The System and achieving greatness. Oftentimes, we look to the physical for success, hoping some new invention or an alteration of technique is going to bring about the change we desire. Sometimes, this is a mistake. You can't always put an exact measurement on the cause of success or attribute it to one factor alone. It can be an intangible and just seem to happen.

This "clicking into place" should not be mistaken for luck though. More often than not, it's due to a deliberate or accidental raise of energy. As immeasurable as it is, there is a rough science to this process. **Feel good and watch your life get better**.

Buzzing

What would happen if you made it your life's mission to feel good?

Ask Lynn Grabhorn. She wrote a book about it called, *Excuse Me, Your Life is Waiting*. Through her stories and insights, she provides an excellent guide on how to develop Soul Power.

Lynn's story is interesting because, throughout her life, she'd been an avid reader of personal development. Interested in anything that might help her experience all life had to offer, she was convinced there must be an underlying theme running throughout the literature that she could use to her benefit. However, after many years of research, she found herself at a dead end.

She'd tried affirmations, visualisations and controlling her thoughts. Although some of these techniques worked for a short while, none of them gave her the breakthrough she sought. Eventually, she reached a point where she almost gave up. Maybe it just wasn't possible for a person to transform their life beyond a certain degree. Little did she know; her answer was about to be revealed.

As with all good answers, at first, it seemed too simple to be true. A friend told her that to get the most out of life *she had to develop the ability to control her energy.* She just needed to find a way of living in a positive, uplifted state (something she calls "buzzing") and her external conditions would change to match her inner feeling. It was that simple.

Although the concept appeared simple, putting it into practice proved harder. When Lynn was given this advice, she was in a dire financial situation. Interest rates had changed and this had a massive impact on her mortgage business. Little money was coming in and at the same time, she had to fund a television advertising campaign for a new product she was trying to launch. She was short on money and even shorter on positive energy. However, Lynn was determined to put her friend's advice into practice and set about trying to alter her feelings.

Lynn recorded this struggle in her book. She devised a thirty-day program with the intention of shifting her emotional state from fear to joy.

Making this transition was harder than she expected. One of the main obstacles was remaining positive when bills arrived and she had no means of paying them. She recalls spending entire days in a negative, anxiety ridden state. The depth of this depression surprised her at first. She'd always considered herself to be a bubbly, positive person. It was only when she began to develop a greater awareness of her energy, she realised what lay behind the façade she'd been presenting to the world.

Despite the initial disappointment, Lynn continued with the practise of building her energy. After a tumultuous couple of weeks, she made a breakthrough; reaching the stage where she spent most of the day feeling upbeat. When she took it a step further and really began to buzz, the results were astounding. She documented a massive improvement in her creative capacities which subsequently led to greater wealth and a more enjoyable life. The next section, taken from the book, highlights part of this change:

> The more I buzzed, the more business I'd get, so I'd buzz even more. It was magic. The money was flowing in so fast, I actually stopped counting. Running my energy became such a routine pastime, I could almost forecast how much business would come in by the intensity and frequency of my buzzing. . . .
>
> Everywhere I turned, it was as if it were my time. There was a ripe and ready market which I knew I could tap with ease. The little flyers I inserted into the newspaper were so effective my phone would ring with loan appointments for weeks afterwards. No matter where I looked, things were extraordinarily positive, and of course, so were my vibrations. My energy level was off the charts, my social life was thriving, and my ancient wardrobe sprouted anew from carefree shopping sprees, all while my business boomed. And before the year was out, I had even launched a new enterprise totally separate from the mortgage business. I just kept unconsciously observing the good stuff all around me, running my energy and pulling in more. How good could it get!?[20]

This process sounds easy, almost too good to be true. Just feel great all day long and the rest of your life will fall into place. As Lynn says, *"How good could it get!?"*

While you shouldn't view Lynn's story with scepticism, a note of caution must be struck. Mastering this new skill is a long-term transition. Just because you're buzzing now, it doesn't mean your life is going to change overnight. Remember, it's not just about feeling great today; you've got to do it tomorrow and the next day, and then the one after that. The process is on-going and just as certainly as buzzing will bring great opportunities into your life; a lack of energy will do the reverse.

For Lynn, the transition was made possible by avoiding negative thoughts. Possibly like you, she faced a mountain of issues that included debt and time-consuming commitments to other people and businesses. Trying to buzz while living in the reality of these issues proved impossible. Therefore, she had to do something to take her mind off the situation.

To do this, she substituted negative thoughts with positive ones. Sometimes it was an ambition she had or a desire to achieve a certain goal. On other occasions, it was the thought of owning a house by the lake and occasionally, it was an appreciation of the beauty of life. She was persistent with these thoughts. *She absolutely would not let herself dwell on the negatives.* For her, this was as dangerous as walking in front of a bus.

You would do well to approach your own negative states with a similar level of caution. Treat them for what they are - potentially life destroying – and refuse to dwell on them. While they're not going to result in your immediate death, they *will* rob you of the energy and vitality needed to deal with your issues.

To counter this threat, and boost your energy at any given time, you'll have to find the thoughts and images that enable you to buzz. Simply feeling ok, or even feeling good, is not enough. You have to become dynamic; you have to feel the excitement of how your life is going to be.

Approaching life with this kind of intensity may seem odd, but this is how we *should* be living. For too long The System has robbed us of our vitality and deceived us into thinking life is a routine struggle interspersed with a few moments of joy. As a result, we're dead to the idea our lives could be an adventure. In a world full of commitments, obligations and predictability, it seems strange, almost fantasy like. However, if you wish to make use of the power of your feelings and develop your Soul Power, you have to open your mind to this possibility.

After all, this is your one experience of life, your one shot at greatness. It should be lived with an emotion that reflects the opportunity you've been given.

Good Vibrations

The title of Lynn Grabhorn's book (*Excuse Me, Your Life is Waiting*) perfectly summarises the excitement of Soul Power. The life of your dreams is now within your grasp, separated only by energy and emotion. Previous to reading this chapter, you may have thought it impossible that such intangible qualities could have a *real* impact on your life. However, now you're aware of the "master secret of the ages," perhaps you also realise "reality" is not all it seems.

Far from being the barrier that blocks the realisation of your dreams, it is a malleable matter that responds to your own energy.

To mould this matter, though, you'll need an in-depth knowledge of your inner world. Many of us are good at putting on a brave face and appearing cheerful. However, to live with Soul Power, this won't cut it.

Genuine positive energy can't be faked. You're going to have to find out what really gets you excited. In making this discovery, you'll also find out one of the greatest benefits of living with Soul Power – *success can be effortless*. Contrary, to what you've been taught, a life of greatness does not equate to one long hard struggle. When you're buzzing at the right frequency, success will come without having to worry over every little outcome. **Keep rising, and everything will fall into place.**

Chapter 8
How to Rise above your Present Environment

Living with Soul Power requires two great shifts in your understanding of life. The first, covered in the previous chapter, is about viewing your reality as a reflection of your inner state. The second, covered in this chapter, is the realisation your circumstances and environment cannot constrain you in any way.

The ancient Greek philosopher, Epictetus, once said, "*Men are disturbed not by things, but by the view which they take of them.*" This insight gets to the core of the shift in understanding you must undergo. Your circumstances and conditions, no matter how desperate, can no longer be seen as a block to your advance. In fact, you can achieve greatness no matter where you've come from or at what point you now stand.

Conditions be Damned

One of the greatest difficulties of liberating yourself from The System is bridging the gap between your present environment and the one you want to create. It's likely there are many areas of your life you're unhappy with. Perhaps it's a lack of money, the frustration at not knowing what you want to do with your life, a boring job, uninspiring colleagues and friends, poor living conditions, a demanding boss, bad health, a dysfunctional relationship or a drug and alcohol addiction. The list could be endless and, in most cases, these problems combine to drain your energy.

This is bad news. The previous chapter looked at the importance of energy in relation to environment and drew a simple but profound conclusion – low energy people aren't equipped with the dynamism needed to escape The System. You need to be buzzing with Soul Power to convince people of your ideas, have the motivation to work daily on your dream and perform to the best of your ability. How is this possible when your energy is constantly knocked by an environment you feel out of harmony with?

The short answer is it's not and that's why another mental discipline must be mastered to continue your advance. I call it the "skill of detachment" and it requires you to remain emotionally detached from the negativity of your present environment. Mastering this discipline means embracing Epictetus's philosophy. You have to realise nothing in your reality has the power to permanently influence your energy. While negative events may rock you, and an uninspiring environment may provide a reminder that you are not where you want to be, neither of them has the power shut down your inspiration. Embracing this philosophy will give you the space needed to develop your Soul Power unhindered by the mental monotony of life in The System. It will also lead you to a profound understanding that will assist you throughout your journey to greatness – *you have power over your conditions.*

As much as The System wants you to believe that certain situations are unalterable and you are shackled to the role it has given you, this will only be the case if you allow your circumstances to affect you. The important thing to remember is you have a choice. No matter how difficult life may be for you at the moment, you can decide to focus on your energy and not your surroundings.

Ultimately, this decision will revolutionise your life. Making a shift from viewing your present environment as something that dictates your outlook, to a changeable point in your life, frees you from the grip of The System. If it's not your lack of money, contacts, experience in your chosen field or success that's getting you down, *but the meaning you give to this predicament,* then this is something you can change. By giving it a meaning that permits the continuation of your journey, you prove to yourself no situation has the power to constrain you.

Rewriting your Story

One of the best ways to detach from the negativity of your present environment is to rewrite your story. This technique is often referred to as reframing and involves creating a new, positive meaning for your situation. Even if you're struggling with mounting debts, or facing rejection after rejection, you change the narrative in such a way that gives you the energy to move forward.

Before I guide you through the process of rewriting *your* story, let me first give you an example. I frequently used this technique with my hypnotherapy clients. One such client, Claire, had dreams of becoming a professional singer. While we initially worked on removing performance anxiety when singing, she also suffered with feelings of helplessness when it came to taking the steps necessary to realise her dream. I will now recall her story and the reframe we used to make sense of her struggle.

Claire worked a low-level role in a bank. She didn't enjoy the job but did it to support herself and her young child. In the little spare time she had, she attempted to break into the music industry. She had vocal training, booked studio time and gigged up and down the country. She put her soul into this pursuit and received some encouraging feedback from a few talent scouts.

While chasing her dream, though, the problems were mounting. Claire was permanently frustrated with her job and felt isolated by the twin endeavour of raising her child alone and pursuing her dream to be a singer. She felt like it was her against the world and when she looked into the future all she could see were years of hardship and struggle.

As a result of this interpretation, Claire felt drained of any positive energy. The only time she felt good was when making progress with her music. The rest of the time she felt overwhelmed. She explained she owed it to herself to try and pursue her dream, but because most of her focus was on the obstacles, she was starting to doubt she could make it.

Obviously, with this understanding of her situation, she never would. My advice was to rewrite her story in a way that both made sense of the hardships she had to endure, and got her feeling more positive about the direction her life was heading.

We started by reframing her job in the bank. It was now to become the foundation of her career as a singer. I stressed how it took care of the essentials for her and her daughter and, therefore, provided a platform to aim at greatness. With such an interpretation she would give those endless hours spent in the bank a meaning. They were now part of the bigger picture. As a result, her time spent at work would be imbued with a new sense of purpose.

When dealing with the struggle of raising a daughter on her own, we reframed it as preparation for her future career. We agreed any person who makes it in the music industry has to be strong. Therefore, the struggle she experienced was a great way of building her character for future success. In this way, a difficult situation was turned into a positive. It wasn't something that was dragging her down, but a means to developing the resilience to conquer any obstacle put before her.

With these new reframes, Claire was able to order her world in a way that removed all feelings of helplessness. Although her life, at times, continued to be a struggle, it now made sense and because of this, was bearable. Not only that, she started to feel excited about the bigger picture. To her, every day was an opportunity to grow and get closer to a new, dream career. As a result, the energy she gave to her singing doubled and she reported a better relationship with her daughter as well.

You'll have to use your reframe in a similar fashion. It has t When creating your reframe, take note of how the new meaning Claire gave her story *presupposed success*. This is the key to using this technique. You have to find a meaning for your present situation that's linked to future success. For Claire, both of the reframes foresaw her becoming a professional a singer. As a result, her mind interpreted everything she was doing as working towards this outcome.

To put you on the path of your dreams and steer you away from the despondency of what could otherwise seem a hopeless situation. For example, losing your job is no longer a reason to panic about how you're going to survive, but an opportunity to find your true purpose in life. Likewise, failing in an attempt to pursue your dreams is no longer evidence your ambitions were unachievable, but an indicator of some area you need to improve. And a failed relationship isn't an example of why you will always be alone but a lesson to learn that will ensure your next one is better.

Even genuinely disastrous news can be interpreted differently. A life-threatening illness or the loss of a loved one, once recovered from, or when the grieving process is complete, can become reasons why you're going to appreciate and make the most of every moment you're given.

All of these examples should give you an idea of how to

re write your story. However, a note of caution must be struck.

While you must wholeheartedly believe in your re-frame, this is not an easy thing to do. Rewriting your story in a way that seems far removed from your day to day life is, initially, uncomfortable. It may feel like you're living a lie and the new perspective you're attempting to adopt bears little relevance to the truth.

If this is the case, there's an important point you must remember. It's not about whether your reframe represents the truth about life, but what it can do for you that counts. It may seem unbelievable that events like losing your job or going bankrupt are now interpreted as opportunities that lead to a greater life. However, if understanding your misfortunes in this way is what it takes to regain your enthusiasm, and develop your Soul Power, then it must be done.

Remember, what we believe to be the truth about ourselves and life is quite often just a perspective. Therefore, you have to ask yourself whether your interpretation is going to help or hinder you. This is what really counts.

Ironically, as you become more successful at rewriting your story, you'll find the thinker/prover mechanism validates your reframe. Whereas before, it acted as a trap, convincing you your negative outlook reflected the truth about life, now, it will do the reverse. By tuning your mind to evidence that validates your reframe, the events and circumstances of your life will only seem to point in a positive direction. Your successes will be viewed as evidence you're heading towards a greater life and your failures will simply highlight areas that need to be improved.

When this occurs, it's a sure sign your subconscious has accepted the new story you've created. You'll have changed the way you perceive your situation and detached yourself from its energy draining influence. What waits on the other side is freedom to enjoy your life *now*.

As powerful as rewriting your story can be, I know there will be some sceptics. They would tell me, and you, that there are some environments and circumstances from which you can *never* escape. Reframing a stressful home life and an uninspiring job is one thing, but what if you have a debilitating illness or are imprisoned against your will?

To these critics, I say the same thing – a person's environment and circumstances DO NOT have the power to define them. However, instead of theory, I now give you examples to prove my point.

The next three cases focus on people who have experienced the most impossible environments yet have been able to overcome their surroundings to attain freedom and greatness. We start with Charlie Chaplin.

Born into abject poverty in Victorian Era London, Chaplin had an exceptionally hard childhood. His father was never around and his mother struggled financially to the point of destitution. Remember, this wasn't 21century "benefits Britain". Poverty in this time often meant starvation (or at least malnutrition) and homelessness or, at best, unhygienic ramshackle housing.

This is the environment Chaplin grew up in. At 14, his

mother was committed to a mental asylum and he was left to fend for himself. This he did, though, and by the time he was 30, he was one of the most famous people in the world with vast wealth, work he loved and the freedom to live life as he chose.

What about imprisonment though? Surely there's no greater evidence of environment constraining an individual than forced detention?

Nelson Mandela as an example of a man whose vision could not be crushed by his environment. Twenty-seven years Mandela spent incarcerated, 18 of them in a cell not much bigger than a toilet cubicle. Work for him was chipping away at rocks in a quarry and family time was one 30 minute visit each a year. How soul destroying must this environment have been?

Fortunately for Mandela, South Africa, and the world, though, he had a reframe that gave him the strength to endure these hardships and eventually rise above them. In his mind, he wasn't trapped in a living hell without any hope of release (his original sentence was life). Instead, he was spiritually connected to a movement for the freedom and empowerment of an entire people. It was alive within him, and it was alive outside the prison walls in which he dwelt. This knowledge gave him a positive outlook that prevented him giving into despondency and a hatred that could have blinded his keen political judgement. Eventually, his environment could no longer contain him. A system that was thought to have absolute power over his body crumbled around the strength of his spirit.

The final example provides perhaps the greatest evidence that a person's environment does not have the power to stop them. Viktor Frankl was held captive in a Nazi concentration camp for 3 years. Whilst detained, he experienced a starvation diet, hard physical labour, exposure to the cold, sleep deprivation, unhygienic living conditions and the death of those around him. In his book, *Man's Search for Meaning*, he estimated the environment he was living in gave him a one in twenty chance of survival. That's not a one in twenty chance of living a happy life. Rather, his environment was so harsh that to just physically stay alive was very unlikely.

But he didn't die. He outlived his environment and went onto to have a successful career as a psychologist and sold over 9 million copies of his most famous book. How was this possible?

Interestingly, Frankl's solution is very similar to the concept of rewriting your story. He claims the tiny minority who survived the Nazi concentration camps did so because they found a meaning for their life. His was based on the important work he planned on doing when freed from the concentration camp, his love for his family and wife and his determination to face imprisonment without losing his dignity and humanity. This not only gave him hope for the future, but enabled him to make sense of the suffering he experienced. He was fond of quoting Nietzsche who famously said, *"He who has a why to live for can bear almost any how."*

All of these examples provide evidence that your spirit plays a more important role in determining your life than your environment. This is worth bearing in mind as you continue your journey to escape The System.

Often, you might feel faced with an impossible situation.

You may feel your environment is so out of harmony with where you want to be, that you lack motivation to take the action necessary to get there. It's pointless. It's hopeless. That voice in your head will reel off a stream of negative self-talk that can quickly convince you there's little to be done.

Now, though, you take a different approach. You realise your environment responds to your energy and this is why it's so important to detach from one that influences you negatively. While you may not be able to immediately escape, or up roots and leave, you can begin reframing the meaning of what you experience. If done successfully, this will grant you the energy needed to begin acting on your plan to escape The System.

Before we leave this subject, there's one more area we must explore. The benefits of mastering the skill of detachment stretch beyond the ability to conquer your environment.

Throughout your journey to greatness, you will be faced with key pressure moments. Perhaps it's an interview for an important job, a single match that, if won, will see you make a breakthrough in your sporting career or an examination of any kind. There are many times in our lives when we have to run the metaphorical gauntlet and give the best of ourselves when it appears everything is on the line.

I want you prepared when these moments occur. Read on to discover the ideal mind set to overcome performance anxiety, fear of failure and complacency when experiencing success.

Triumph and Disaster

Winning is everything (or so we've been led to believe). Every day, we see images of famous people achieving sporting, political and business victories. We hear of friends and colleagues who have just gained promotion or closed a deal. We look in the history books and read about famous conquerors whose triumphs shaped the direction of humanity.

Added to this, we are raised in a system that places a huge level of importance on the material. Our value is largely determined by what we own. The size of our property, the expense of our car, the clothes we wear, how much we get paid and the status attached to our job, all go into creating a value for ourselves we and others believe in. These are all usually achieved through personal victories. As a result, it wouldn't be too far-fetched to say that winning (or losing) makes us who we are.

As crucial as winning is, though, it can't be achieved with this kind of attitude. Ironically, believing winning is everything might actually work against you and sabotage your chances of success. This is the key message you must learn. *As important as advancing your life is, you have to maintain a level of detachment from all outcomes, to do so.*

The reason for this is the difficulty in achieving a high energy state when consumed by the daily possibilities of success and failure. It destabilises you. One minute you're up (when receiving good news), the next minute you're down (when a decision goes against you). Progressively moving your life forwards, against the background of a permanently fluctuating inner state, is virtually impossible. Instead, you have to remain detached. As difficult as it may be to separate yourself from outcomes that could seemingly change your life, you must always maintain your composure.

The importance of adopting this approach can't be underestimated. Ironically, it's what gives you the winning edge. If you're able to maintain the same inner state, whether achieving goals, or dealing with setbacks, your forwards momentum will continue. This is because your energy is not dependent on the whims of your physical reality. Where many people become complacent with success, and crumble when faced with defeat, you'll maintain your focus throughout.

Perhaps the best example of the skill of detachment can be seen with the former tennis champion Bjorn Borg. Known as the "Ice Man," he invariably performed to the best of his abilities. When on court it was difficult to tell whether he was winning or losing. The same impassive expression was adopted when hitting a winner or making a mistake. He appeared focused on each point and concerns about the scoreboard never seemed to register.

This ability to detach himself from outcomes was never more evident than in the 1980 Wimbledon Final. In this match he faced John McEnroe and a date with destiny. Pursuing his fifth Wimbledon title in a row, at the time a record, he found himself tested to the limit. He was leading 2 sets to 1 and all that stood between him and the Championship was a fourth set tie breaker.

Usually this would involve a first to seven-point shootout. However, in this match, the tie break exceeded all expectations.

Lasting 20 minutes, and containing some fantastic shot making, each player had chances to claim the decisive blow. In total, Borg squandered seven match points. He was within one point of history on seven occasions but was unable to cross the line. Instead, after many missed opportunities of his own, McEnroe finally claimed the tie breaker and the fourth set by 18 points to 16.

For Borg, this should have been the end of the match. To be within one point of victory (on seven separate occasions) and fail, should have been enough to break him. How could he possibly find the strength to win the decisive final set when all of the momentum was now with McEnroe? Malcolm Folley, in his book, *Borg vs. McEnroe,* describes what happened next:

At the moment he surrendered the tie – break, Borg dropped the second ball he was holding and trudged to his chair. He walked so heavily he could have been wearing diving boots. He was lost in his own bleak world and deaf to the cacophony on the Centre Court. Dan Maskell, the doyen of the BBC commentary team, watched on his monitor as the director summoned a close up of the Swede. "What must Bjorn be thinking?" asked Maskell. And that was the point. No one ever knew. But years later Bjorn admitted, "I think I never felt so bad in my life. That was the worst moment I had since I was born. Losing seven match points . . .playing my fifth Wimbledon final . . .against John McEnroe . . .so I think I am going to lose this match. I mean I had no chance."

But Borg was not a man to wallow in his own stupor

for long. Like the champion he is, he found a higher gear from nowhere. McEnroe lost the next four points, three of them to winners from Borg. The game belonged to the Swede. Bergelin [his coach] looked on with a mixture of disbelief and awe. "For me, it was the most fantastic thing that Bjorn could come back after the fourth set. He showed the fighter he is – and after all those match balls, too! He never gave up. He thinks over what is going on. He thinks only of the next ball. Finally, he finds himself."[21]

Borg went on to win the final set 8 – 6, cementing his place in history as the first, and at the time, only man to have won 5 consecutive Wimbledon titles. It was a feat made even more extraordinary by the manner in which it was achieved. To have squandered seven opportunities to claim his prize, and still have the composure to rally himself for the final set, displayed an extraordinary level of detachment from the outcome he desired.

To put this into perspective, imagine a goal you want above all else and then imagine that you are within one step of achieving it. Then, imagine it slips through your fingers seven times, leaving you to regroup, double your efforts and pursue your goal all over again. Would you feel frustrated? Would you be able to maintain your positive energy?

Borg could, and his example contains an important lesson about greatness. Being able to detach yourself from the emotion of the moment is vital. Your energy can't be dictated by what's going on around you. Instead, you have to regulate your own energy levels, keeping your enthusiasm and motivation at a peak.

To do this, you can't think about the possibility of victory or defeat. Remove all thought of both outcomes from your mind. Instead, adopt the Borg approach and metaphorically *"think only of the next ball."*

This helped Borg because he didn't play the fifth set thinking he'd just blown one of the greatest opportunities in his life. Instead, he played it by focusing on one shot at a time and allowed the result to take care of itself.

And it did. His coach remarks how, *"Finally, he finds himself"* during the final set. This means that he was able to unleash his true potential - the ultimate prize of mastering the skill of detachment. Ask yourself, "How many times have you left an important contest, meeting or occasion *knowing* you could have performed better than you did?" Many people live with the feeling they have so much more to give. Sadly, this potential may only reveal itself when the pressure is off and nothing is at stake. However, when it counts, and the possibilities of success or failure are very real, it gets locked away.

The skill of detachment shows you how to bring this potential out. By focusing purely on maintaining your Soul Power, and not the outcome you wish to achieve, you'll be primed to give the best of yourself in any situation.

If

Whether Borg was born with a naturally detached disposition, or whether he developed it with time, is not clear. However, it's definitely a skill *you* can develop.

Ironically, one of the keys to doing so is inscribed above the entrance to Centre Court at Wimbledon. Here, written on a plaque, are two lines from the famous Rudyard Kipling poem, *If.* These lines explain the new understanding you must adopt. Separated from the poem at large, they read as follows,

> If you can meet with Triumph and Disaster
> And treat those two impostors just the same;

Although brief, these words capture the essence of the skill of detachment. You must develop a new understanding of success and failure. Previously, you may have viewed these two occurrences as end points. Triumph signals a time for celebration, disaster a point of defeat that prompts feelings of inadequacy and despair. In both cases, these opposite ends of the achievement spectrum signify finality. The win means your job is done. The loss means your chances for success are over.

To perform to the best of your ability, though, this understanding has to change. You have to see your life as a continuation rather than a series of end points. This is what Kipling meant when he referred to Triumph and Disaster as "imposters." He wanted you to realise these two experiences are *reactions* to a much greater power. It's a reminder you must focus on what brings success and not obsess over success itself. Belief in your abilities and the ability to raise your energy, directed towards a dream created by your inspiration (rather than the values The System imposes on you) is the greater power that creates all success. Worship your daily commitment to focus on these qualities, rather than getting emotionally overawed by outcomes, and your progress will be assured.

With this new understanding, a world of opportunity is now within reach. While most people will waste their energy becoming over excited by success and dejected by defeat, you'll remain constant throughout. You'll keep moving towards your overall objective, and without the ups and downs, the speed at which you'll achieve your goals will be greatly enhanced. You won't get complacent when experiencing success and you won't give up when faced with defeat. As Kipling says at the end of his poem:

> Yours is the Earth and everything that's in it
> And – which is more – you'll be a man, my son!

The Battle Within

Mastering the skill of detachment is simple. Stop worrying about environment and outcome and instead, focus on your energy. If you ever find yourself thinking, "will that important decision go my way, will that man or woman I like message me back, will I get enough sleep if I have something important to do the next day or will I get enough clients this week?" then take a step back from these thoughts. Detach yourself and charge your energy to a level where you are continually buzzing. It's really that simple. All it takes is awareness and discipline.

As simple as it is, though, its importance must not be overlooked. The System will attempt to convince you that your life is an external battle. It wants you to believe environment and the outcome of events are everything.

While on the surface, they may appear to be so, there's a much more important, and deeper, battle taking place.

This is the battle for your thoughts and feelings and whether you can master them, or whether they will run away with you. Achieving this mastery could be described as the "Ultimate Boon" Joseph Cambell references in his Heroes Journey analogy. *It's your superpower*. Take it into the world and create the change you want to see.

Chapter 9
Why Controlling your Life doesn't work and what you need to do Instead

As well as informing you on the steps necessary to attaining freedom and greatness, I need to make you aware of the pitfalls. The System's influence is rarely positive and it's at its most destructive when conditioning you to exert control over your life. It will encourage you to struggle, fret and fight your way to success. It wants you to believe progress won't occur unless you force it through.

This approach is the by-product of living in a system that burdens you with numerous demands. Every day you have to be at a certain place at a certain time. You have to meet targets and your performance is constantly being monitored and assessed. Are you good enough? It's a question you have to wrestle with throughout your life and the answer often leads to deep seated insecurities.

Added to this, you have to contend with The System's relentless pace. John Lennon once said, "*Life is what happens while you are busy making other plans.*" You're so consumed by dealing with the day to day reality of paying the bills, the mortgage, looking after the kids and commitments at work, that although you may plan to do so much, your aspirations often get sacrificed for the sake of survival.

How do you exist in a reality like this? The obvious answer would appear to be through *control*. If you can exert the maximum amount of influence over your actions, behaviour, responses, opinions, and if you can mould yourself into what The System wants you to be, then maybe you'll survive or become a success.

If you've adopted this approach, though, you'll realise you won't. At best, you'll be able to function - holding down a job, paying your bills and having enough money to enjoy a holiday each year. However, the price you pay for living in this fashion is an almost unbearable amount of stress and tension.

This occurs because you're fighting against something. In an attempt to succeed through exerting control, you're ignoring your inner voice and overlooking an easier approach to attaining success.

Hitting Bottom

Hitting bottom isn't a weekend retreat. It's not a god damn seminar. Stop trying to control everything and just let go. LET GO!

-Tyler Durden, *Fight Club*

Fight Club is about a man learning to let go. The main character, Jack, is frustrated with life in The System. He hates his job, is unable to sleep, has become obsessed with buying catalogue furniture and attends support groups for the terminally ill. In short, he's lost. He's bought into The System but is completely dissatisfied with what it offers. Subconsciously, he searches for a way out. He doesn't know what he's looking for but he needs to escape a life devoid of adventure and meaning.

Jack finds this way out through a chance encounter with the film's other main character, Tyler Durden. They meet on a plane and Jack is quickly impressed by the charismatic Tyler. His approach to life is the complete antithesis of Jack's. He works a series of odd jobs and makes and sells soap. Living in an abandoned house, in a deserted part of town, there should be no reason for Jack to be envious of his existence. However, despite his material advantages, Jack longs to be like Tyler.

This longing is born out of the freedom Tyler enjoys. Tyler's creed can be summed up by a few sentences: "*I say never be complete, I say stop trying to be perfect. I say let's evolve . . .and let the chips fall where they may.*" Tyler doesn't feel the need to control. He knows who he is and is confident in his abilities. As a result, he can allow life to take its course. He's not interested in material possessions, making money or playing The System's game. What appeals to him is the constant evolution of his life and the concept of "hitting bottom."

"Hitting bottom" is an intriguing philosophy. Tyler's main premise is you must "let go" of every impulse to control your life. Instead, *you allow it to happen.* You're open to the moment and ever ready to explore where your inspiration leads.

This philosophy scares Jack at first. He's been raised to always stay in control and care about things The System tells him are important. However, as the film progresses, he realises Tyler's philosophy is not about unrestrained anarchy.

Instead, Tyler's showing him how to live a life where the insignificant events (losing a job you hate, the quest for material wealth and other people's criticisms) aren't able to dull his spirit. More important than these would be tragedies is to know how it feels to be *alive*, and Jack learns never to lose sight of this awareness.

At present, you may feel your life couldn't function without control. Where would your motivation come from? Without forcing it, would your desire for success even exist? Occasionally you may want to, but you simply can't turn your back on The System's demands. Your life would fall apart. Or would it . . .

My role is to be the Tyler Durden in your life. I'm going to introduce you to a way of living that removes struggle and stress and puts you on the path to effortless success.

If you've ever failed to realise your potential in a creative, professional or sporting endeavour, are constantly worried about the future or struggle with basic functions like sleeping, sex and constipation, then it's for a reason. You've lost a connection with the part of yourself that can solve all of these problems without exerting any conscious effort.

We'll now explore how to reconnect. You need to;

- Stop worrying about outcomes and whether they will go your way.
- Stop overthinking your problems and *trying* to find a solution.
- Stop forcing your body to do what you want it to do.

Instead, LET GO and TRUST that everything is going to work out the way you want. Do nothing at all. While The System spurs you into action with words like "must" "emergency" "maximum effort" and "take action," I'm telling you to let it all go. Stop forcing, and let the answer or solution *come* to you. Here's why.

In chapter 5 we established that belief determines everything. It doesn't matter whether what you believe in is "true" or "false," belief in an outcome (if strong enough) will make it come to pass.

If you accept this premise, then ask yourself this question, "How much belief am I displaying if I have to control an outcome, solution or function?" The answer is, "none at all." If you have to force and exert effort it reveals an underlying doubt in the possibility of achieving what you desire. The tension is born of uncertainty. Therefore, in a world governed by the power of belief, what will happen when your efforts to achieve something are powered by doubt?

This is why trying to control an outcome often brings about the reverse of what you intended. While your desire is strong, your intentions are good and your strategy might be sound, if, deep down, you doubt the success of your endeavour, the tension you display in your efforts to achieve it will sabotage your attempts.

This happens because you are operating from a mindset of lack. How much faith do you show if you constantly have to worry and force the outcomes you desire? Surely if you believe something will occur then you are relaxed and confident, certain in the knowledge you will achieve your goal? This is why letting go is the perfect approach to achieving greatness. It puts you in the right frame of mind to attract success.

I would understand if you are sceptical. How could letting go connect you with answers that will reveal a path to a greater life, ensure you perform to the best of your ability and guarantee harmony in all your basic functions? It almost seems absurd, but what you must remember is that letting go is the basic demand of every religion. Whether it's Christianity, Islam or Buddhism, the devotee is called upon to have *faith* in the idea the power they worship wants a good, happy and meaningful life for them. In, *The Bible*, Jesus is reported as saying, *"take no thought for the morrow"* and St. Paul advises us to be, *"careful in nothing."* You have to live with a belief that your solution will be found and you will have everything you want.

Wayne Dyer also echoed these thoughts. In his book, *The Wisdom of the Ages*, he referred to the process of "Letting go and Letting God." Trust in God/The Universe, by releasing all worry and doubt, and your faith will be rewarded with the outcome you desire. It's that simple. The only thing stopping you living the life you want is failure to control thoughts of doubt, lack and fear.

Even a lack of religious faith won't stop this principle from working. That's because it's not the worship of God that permits this principle to work, but a proper understanding of how the Universe works. **When you realise that The Universe/The Creator/your subconscious mind/Infinite Intelligence/God (or whatever you want to call the power that gives life) is on your side and always urging you towards a life of harmony, brilliance and love, then you can be certain that letting go will work.** Therefore, your role is one of preventing self-sabotage rather than playing the ranting coach, screaming at his players from the side-line.

The 3 rules for activating this power are as follows.

1. Stop worrying about problems.
2. Stop overthinking/trying to find solutions.
3. Stop forcing your body to do what you want it to do.

Prove to yourself that the letting go principle works. Become your own scientist and run your own experiments. I promise you the changes you'll experience will be little short of amazing.

Imagine a life where you don't have to worry where the money to pay the mortgage is coming from, you just believe it will come, stay active, and somehow it arrives. Imagine a life where you don't have to stress about creating content for your YouTube channel or blog, you just immerse yourself in your field and somehow ideas pop into your head. Imagine a life where you don't have to force your golf swing or tennis serve into what you think it should be, you just learn all you can about the technique and allow your body to find its way to the perfect shot. All of this and more is waiting when you learn to let go of the need to control.

A great analogy to explain the transformation you are about to undergo can be found by returning to *Fight Club*. (Warning: Spoiler Alert. If you haven't watched the film and plan on doing so then you might want to skip to the next section). About three quarters of the way through the film Jack discovers that he *is* Tyler Durden. Previously, he believed Tyler was his mentor but after a series of strange coincidences, he finally realises that he is, in fact, his alter ego. Like the classic comic book model, they have a civilian and superhero mode. While attempting to control his life, Jack takes over. When able to let go and hit bottom, Tyler comes out to play.

The differences between these two sides of the same character are vast and demonstrate the rewards of letting go. As Tyler says to Jack when he finally realises they are the same person, "*All the ways you wish you could be – that's me. I look like you want to look; I fuck like you want to fuck. I'm smart, capable and most importantly, I'm free in all the ways that you are not.*"

A Lesson in Letting Go

I'll now share with you part of the transformation that occurred to me through learning to let go. I was introduced to the concept, and began my journey, as a result of dealing with a particularly bad case of insomnia. The following story recalls my experiences and demonstrates both the ineffectiveness of trying to force the outcomes you desire, and the effortless manner in which letting go can change your life.

Throughout my life, I'd never been a great sleeper. I'd suffered from patches of insomnia as a child but nothing compared to the experience I had while at university. It was here, during a long summer break, I experienced my worst bout of this insufferable condition.

Some insomniacs find it impossible to fall asleep but for me this wasn't the case. My difficulties came 3 to 4 hours after I'd drift off. It was then I'd suddenly wake and find myself unable to get back to sleep. After only a week of sleeping in this fashion, my lack of rest began to take its toll. I'd go to my summer job already feeling exhausted. This feeling continued well into the day and was usually accompanied by pains in my head, ears or around my eyes. As a result, I could barely function and enjoyable hobbies like playing tennis became a chore. Worst of all, I found myself inhabiting a zombie like state. I was never fully awake, yet never long asleep and always low on energy. After only a few days of living this way, I was desperate for some kind of relief.

Unfortunately, at that point in my life, all I knew how to do was *force* myself back to sleep. I would repeat an affirmation over in my mind, telling myself, "I am falling asleep, I am falling asleep," hoping it would have the desired effect. If that didn't work, I'd just lie there; trying to *make* myself feel tired. Using my mind, I'd try to generate a heavy feeling throughout my body, attempting to trigger some kind of sleep response.

When this failed, I became increasingly frustrated and questioned why it was I couldn't get back to sleep. Each night saw the emergence of a different theory. Maybe it was something from my childhood, maybe there was a lesson I needed to learn, maybe I was being punished or maybe this was just my new sleeping pattern. I would lie there, thinking all these thoughts, desperately trying to figure it out but never finding an answer that would permit me to sleep.

As the weeks passed by, and there was still no reprieve, my life became dominated by insomnia. I was so focused on my lack of sleep I became obsessed with my condition. I spent the days trying to convince myself that each night would be the one where I'd finally sleep peacefully. Then, I'd spend the nights engaged in a losing battle, tossing and turning and worrying about how exhausted I was going to feel the next day.

In an attempt to trick my mind into breaking this pattern, I changed my sleeping times, moved the position of my bed, bought lavender scented pillows (supposedly designed to induce sleep) and got sleeping pills from the doctor. However, none of these provided anything more than a temporary release and it wasn't long before I'd reached my breaking point.

Words of Wisdom

Years later, after I became a hypnotherapist, I discovered that many people used my services as a last resort. They had to be desperate and have exhausted every possibility before they would finally call.

This shouldn't have surprised me, though, because I was exactly the same. Having felt I'd tried everything, when someone suggested I should see a hypnotherapist, I jumped at the chance. Not knowing what to expect, I went into the session with an open mind. What I was to learn drastically improved my ability to sleep and also provided me with an insight that would change my life forever.

When I first walked into the hypnotherapist's office, I was full of expectation. I was so desperate to overcome my insomnia I was willing to try anything. Prepared for an out of body experience, or at least to be under the control of this mysterious figure, I was taken back by the fact that we just talked for 30 minutes. However, there was a reason for this approach, as through his line of questioning; he began to unravel the peculiarities of my problem.

While we talked, the hypnotherapist asked me various questions and gained an insight into my insomnia. Then, towards the end of our conversation, he informed me that he slept perfectly and asked me how I thought he approached the subject of sleep.

Slightly confused, I told him that I had no idea. He responded by saying this was precisely the point; he *didn't* have an approach. Sleep came naturally to him; it wasn't something he had to force. Slightly irritated, I asked him why it didn't just "happen" for me. He smiled and informed me that it was because I *did* have an approach.

From our 30-minute conversation, it was clear to him I was trying to control my sleeping habits. The repeating of affirmations, the trying to make myself feel tired and the attempts at finding an answer that would allow me to rest, were all signs of a person who was trying to *force* themselves to sleep. Rather than being a natural function, guided by my subconscious mind, my sleeping habits had become something I directly attempted to control. I was putting all this stress and effort into a function that should come naturally. How could I expect to sleep properly when following this approach?

Interested by this explanation, I was keen to know the solution. He explained that if I was able to let go of the need to control, and my fear of not being able to sleep, then my bodies' natural sleeping mechanism would soon take over. However, I had to *completely* let go.

There was no room for internal dialogues or attempts to convince myself I could sleep peacefully. This would only add fuel to the fire that had become my obsession with sleep. Instead, I had to let go of that addictive urge to manipulate the outcome. Only by doing this, would I let the greater wisdom of my subconscious mind step in and take over.

After this explanation, the hypnotherapist induced a state of trance and conveyed this message to my subconscious. In a relaxed state, between sleep and full consciousness, I felt his words take effect. When I opened my eyes, it was with a renewed sense of hope. We agreed to book a follow up session but I felt certain I wouldn't need it.

Despite my optimism, and some initially positive results, the wisdom of his words didn't take immediate effect. I found it difficult to completely let go of my need to control. Upon waking in the middle of the night, I was still tempted (and sometimes did) use all of my old tactics to try to get back to sleep. It just seemed like the best approach to take. I was still convinced I had to fight and overcome my insomnia. How could it improve by doing nothing at all?

With this question in mind, I booked another session. Pleased with the progress I'd made, but not yet sleeping as

I should, I was keen for the hypnotherapist to elaborate on the concept of letting go. I told him I couldn't let go of my need to control when I felt the situation was unresolved. Furthermore; I mentioned that letting go felt a bit like quitting. How was I supposed to walk away from an issue that dominated my life when I had no answer on *how* it was going to be solved?

Throughout my explanation, the hypnotherapist had been listening intently and when he replied, it was clear he'd been expecting these questions. **He explained that the need to control can make letting go feel like giving up.** However, I was not to make the mistake of thinking that's what I was doing.

He informed me that letting go when you don't have an answer to your problem actually requires a great deal of bravery. It's not weakness but strength. It displays a belief in your ability to achieve your desire because you don't have to *force* the outcome to happen. You *know* it will happen and as a result, you can rest peacefully in this knowledge. Therefore, letting go didn't mean I was doing nothing. Instead, I was actually displaying a belief in my ability to sleep.

After the hypnotherapist gave me this explanation, I knew he was right and couldn't wait to put the concept into practice. However, before I got carried away, he struck a cautionary note.

He explained that although I may have felt I understood the theory, it was a concept I'd only truly grasp *after* I'd put it into practice. This is because an answer wouldn't come to me instantly. I had to let go and take a leap of faith *first*. Without the illusion of control to hold onto, I had to believe I could sleep properly. Only then, would I gain the clarity to find a solution.

With these parting words, I felt truly prepared to deal with my insomnia. I left feeling certain I'd be able to identify any attempt to control my sleep and let go. Then, I assumed, it would just be a matter of time before my sleeping habits returned to normal.

Although it wasn't all plain sailing, my recovery was almost as smooth as I'd imagined. Fortunately, the ability to let go operated much like a skill. The more I practised it, the better I got. What made a real difference was letting go of the dread I experienced when thinking about the prospect of a bad night's sleep. This used to be especially powerful when I had something important to do the next day. For example, if I had a tennis match, I'd think to myself, "I've got to sleep well tonight or I'm not going to have the energy to perform tomorrow," or "I couldn't bear it if I'm tired again for my game." These thoughts would send a wave of anxiety through me as I contemplated the likelihood of them occurring. On almost all occasions, they created a self-fulfilling prophecy.

However, as soon as I began to let go, I experienced a change. *Because I didn't allow myself to dwell on the issue, or try to convince myself I'd sleep well*, I found the fear gradually subsided. Whereas before, I'd go to bed feeling very anxious; now, it was like I didn't realise I had something important to do the next day. It was off my radar, out of my consciousness and, as a result, my natural need for sleep took over.

Even when I did wake during the night, I was much better

equipped at dealing with the situation. Before, I might have gritted my teeth in frustration and tried to send myself back to sleep. Now, I didn't even *try*. I just lay there, told myself to let go and waited for the onset of sleep. It took a while but soon I was able to go back to sleep within two hours of waking and then, staying in that drowsy stage between being asleep and awake, I went straight back to sleep.

The Illusion of Control

What makes you believe you need to control your life? Did you have a conscious role in your birth? Did you manufacture the random encounter that led you to meet the love of your life? No, you didn't and yet they still happened.

What's the message here? Control is futile. You are part of a universe with billions of different possibilities and probabilities. You can't manufacture the circumstances and events of your life and, ironically, trying to do so will ensure the outcomes you desire remain even more elusive.

Fortunately, though, you don't need to control your life. As I just mentioned, something as fundamental to your existence as the act of your creation was completely out of your hands and yet it still happened.

Other events fundamental to creating a greater life for yourself will also happen without you needing to consciously force them. My foot into the tennis coaching industry came from a practise partner who happened to know a coach looking for someone to run part of his program. My start in hypnotherapy occurred because, by accident, I was renting a room directly opposite a clinic that offered very fair room rates. This book wouldn't exist if it wasn't for the fact that Tom Butler-Bowdon, an Australian, happened to be living in Oxford, England and I could, therefore, drive to meet him for regular mentoring sessions. The opportunities for living a greater life are all around and you don't need to force them. There's a greater power that orchestrates all of these occurrences but to benefit from it, you have to go with the flow. Try to force a direction or control a path and you may end up denying a much easier and quicker route to your goal.

While the ability to directly control the outcomes of your life is an illusion, there is one area, and one area *only*, that you must exert the utmost control. A rigorous control and direction of your thoughts is absolutely essential. In fact, this is what ensures harmony with the Universe and gives you the best chance of taking advantage of the opportunities that will come your way (and possibly even attracting them).

You must discipline your mind to only think about what you want. Whether that means the perfect romantic relationship, success in your upcoming match or competition or receiving an answer to your problem, you must stay focused on the outcomes you desire. If fear slips in, and your imagination starts presenting outcomes of failure then learn to get a grip of your mind and direct it back to what you want.

Of course, for a large part of your day, you'll need your mind to focus on what you are doing – writing, speaking, listening in a meeting, playing sports, watching a film, reading etc. - and you shouldn't control your thoughts at these times. However, when you have a spare moment, return to this discipline.

Bear in mind that you're engaged in a partnership. You're connected to a greater power that'll help you achieve all of your desires if you'll only do these three things.

1. Direct your thoughts towards what you want to achieve.
2. Stop trying to force external events to go the way you want them.
3. Take action towards the fulfilment of your dream. Please don't interpret my criticism of *forcing* your dreams into reality as meaning you should do nothing at all. If you want to become a writer then you have to sit down and write. You'll also have to research how to improve your writing. Then, once your book is complete, you have to be incredibly proactive in finding an agent or a publisher or promoting yourself online. Just bear in mind, throughout the entire process, not to force it.

Without the need to control, there is a gap that must be filled. If you've been living your life one way (even if it's been unsuccessfully), it will still feel odd to adapt to an existence without control. Will you lose all self-discipline and fall behind your colleagues and peers? Will there be a void where there was once a voice that wouldn't let you slack? What happens when you no longer subscribe to the illusion that we can control every element of our lives? These questions are very important to anybody considering placing their faith in the idea of letting go. We look for more answers in the next chapter.

Chapter 10
How to Connect with your Genius and Overcome fears, doubts and negative thinking

Part of the mystery of my recovery from insomnia was that I never found a set way or routine that allowed me to sleep. It just happened. Besides letting go of my need to control, there wasn't anything I could actually *do*.

This made me wonder about the nature of the power that assisted me. It wasn't something I could directly control. My previous attempts demonstrated the fallacy of this approach. Instead, it seemed to operate by *harmonising with its ways*. If I could adjust to how it wanted me to be, then it would reward me with the outcome I desired.

As I worked with this power in other areas of my life, I experienced similar benefits. The more I let go and the more I believed in my abilities, the more it seemed to help me. It gave me ideas, pointed me in the direction of what I should be doing and enabled me to perform to the best of my abilities. All of these changes occurred *without* my direct control.

Pleased, yet puzzled by this transformation, I was determined to learn more. I wanted to know exactly how this power worked and while watching *Fight Club,* I gained a vital insight.

It came to me in the moment that the plot twist occurs. No longer is Tyler a man who teaches Jack how to "hit bottom" and feel more alive. Instead, he is a part of him that takes over when he releases his need to control.

This made me think about the nature of their relationship. It seemed very confusing until the answer finally hit me. *Tyler is Jack's genie.* He appears when Jack is at his lowest point and literally takes over.

Rather than being summoned by rubbing a lamp, though, Tyler emerges when Jack relinquishes his need to control. Then, like the genie in the tale of Aladdin, he has great power and can transform Jack's life in a way he, as himself, is unable to do.

With this new insight, I started to understand what had replaced my own need to control. Although not a genie from a lamp or an alter ego which I had subconsciously created, it was very similar. It seemed as if I had been touched by a higher intelligence. Had *I cleared a path to my own genius*?

Although such a claim may sound outrageous, personal

experience had changed my opinion of what it meant to possess this power. Previously, I believed that genius was a rare commodity. Perhaps one in a million people could claim it and these lucky few were gifted in a way most of us were not.

This was how I *used* to understand genius and it led me to believe it was a quality you were born with, not something you could *access*. However, when I began to experience the effects of letting go, a new theory developed in my mind. For the first time, I started believing it was possible to be *visited by genius.*

Inviting the Genius

The etymological origins of the word genius reveal something fascinating about the concept. They can be traced back to ancient Rome where the term was used to describe the guiding spirit of a person. Interestingly, this spirit was said to exist in *all* people, visiting them through insights and intuitions. In fact, it spread beyond people to animals and even objects. Everything possessed its own divine nature that could be expressed by the individual.

Compare this with today's understanding of the word, and it's clear to see a great shift has taken place. Now, when we talk about genius, we talk about a quality that's highly exclusive. You have to invent something truly ground-breaking or be head and shoulders above other great people to possess it. As a result, almost all but the smallest percentage of the population is excluded from this category.

Although this view of genius may appear to represent the truth, *you must reject it.* Perhaps it's more than coincidence that the word has now come to represent a quality that is ultra-rare. Could it be The System's conditioning, wanting you to think this way?

Think about it, if you see yourself as an ordinary person then it stops you dreaming you could have something greater than the life The System presents you with. Breaking free would seem far too daunting with your meagre talents and limited ability.

The danger that such a belief could create a self-fulfilling prophecy is why you have to change the way you understand genius. Moving back to the Roman interpretation is more conducive to achieving greatness. This understanding allows for the possibility of you being *visited* by genius, without necessarily *being* a genius.

This is an important distinction. If you live a life you are not satisfied with, the idea that you *are* a genius can appear far-fetched. Your subconscious won't accept it because if you were, then you wouldn't be stuck in your current situation. However, if I was to tell you that you had the potential to be *visited* by genius, then you'd be keen to learn how.

Perhaps you'd remember experiences when it appears you've been touched by a higher power. Whether it expresses itself through a sport you play, an idea that improves your ability work, saying just the right thing at the right time or a hunch that reveals an important answer, I'm certain you can look back and recall such moments. Now, what if you knew how to increase these experiences so that they occurred on a daily basis?

Although conventional wisdom dictates you're either born a genius or not, there's some evidence to suggest otherwise.

One such example is Michael Jackson. On the surface, there was no better case of a bona fide musical genius. With the greatest selling album of all time to his name and a catalogue of hits burned into public consciousness, The System would point to him as a clear case of a person who was born with exceptional abilities. However, when asked his thoughts on the creative process, he had something revealing to say that ran contrary to this notion.

When interviewed, Michael Jackson frequently said it felt like the melodies and lyrics he created came from God. Often, he would wake up with a tune playing in his mind and the song would build itself through this intuition. He then went on to say if he ever sat down and thought, "I'm going to write the greatest selling album of all time" it would never work. The flow would die and he would be left with nothing.

Instead, in one interview he says, "*Don't write the song, let the song write itself,*" and mentions his mentor, Quincy Jones, telling him to get out of the way of the music. (A reference to the idea he should act as a conduit for the music, rather than trying to force it in a certain direction.) These experiences led him to believe that his music was a gift from God.

Of course, most journalists, not understanding what he really meant, took this to be a sign of an over inflated ego. However, I understood it as humility - not feeling he could claim the songs were entirely his work because he felt guided while creating them.

Whatever the case, his thoughts on the creative process are fascinating. Like everyone else, it seems he had to invite his genius. To do this, he had *to listen rather than control.* If he silenced the desire to force out what he hoped to achieve, then he could find a voice that revealed a direction for him to follow.

Interestingly, though, he could still experience the musical equivalent of writers' block. This occurred when he followed his ego and hints at the possibility that rather than just *being* a genius, he had to take steps to *tune* into his power.

As well as providing evidence to dispel The System's genius myth, Michael Jackson also provides an example of what the experience of being visited by genius is like. This can be seen in his 1991 *Dangerous* album sleeve when he gives fans an insight into what happens when he begins to dance.

> On many an occasion when I am dancing, I have felt touched by something sacred. In those moments, I felt my spirit soar and become one with everything that exists. I become the stars and the moon. I become the singer and the song . . .I keep on dancing and then it is the eternal dance of creation. The creator and the creation merge into one wholeness of joy.[22]

These comments reveal what happens in those moments when your intuition reaches a peak and your instincts act on impulse to bring about something special. As Michael Jackson says, it's about, "*the creator and the creation merging into one wholeness of joy.*" Such positive feelings should act as an indicator that a significant discovery or strong connection to your genius is being made. Of course, it's up to you to listen to them, or follow their lead, but such overwhelmingly positive feelings are hard to ignore.

From there, the key is to *trust your subconscious.* Go in the direction it leads, don't try to repeat, relive or over analyse the moment you were visited by genius. Instead, be secure in the knowledge that such moments will always be there to guide you. They may come at the most unexpected of times, but there is no end to them once you learn to let them in.

Everyday Genius

Your genius will reveal itself in a field in which you already specialise or want to learn about. Being visited by this power doesn't always equate to becoming a singing sensation or receiving an idea for a life changing invention. Very simply, genius visits those who are fascinated by what they do. A scientist receives knowledge on how to discover the laws of nature because that's the field in which they operate. Likewise, a sportsman is gifted with extraordinary insight into their game because they practise it day in day out.

You may not be a scientist or sportsman, but by following your inspiration you will find a field in which your particular expertise can flourish. Once you've found this niche, if you are open to your genius, it will reveal the answers you need to excel.

However, remaining open is the key. If you believe The System's genius myth and, as a result, view yourself as insignificant and without talent, then it will be impossible for you to make the connection.

Of course, appropriating a belief in your genius can be a difficult step to take. To make the idea more acceptable, there are two points you must remember. Firstly, you're simply looking for solutions to problems. Secondly, you're searching for a way to excel. As a result, being a genius in The System's eyes is largely irrelevant to your quest. It's not about grandiose displays of brilliance, but specialising to the extent you become a master in your field. Ideally, this will happen to such a degree you almost have no competition. What you do is unique and this places you in great demand.

An example of somebody who embodies this uniqueness, and was able to achieve greatness despite not possessing genius in The System's sense of the word, is Anthony Keidis. Front man of the Red Hot Chilli Peppers, Keidis never lived a conventional life. Growing up in the Hollywood area of Los Angeles, he was introduced to sex, drugs and rock 'n roll at a very early age. However, it was never a given that he would become lead singer of a successful rock band.

Far from it, in fact, as Keidis discusses in his autobiography, *Scar Tissue*. He openly admits not being blessed with one of the world's greatest singing voices.

This caused uncertainty at first because without an obvious natural talent, how was he ever going to break into the music industry? The extract below explains his dilemma.

...seeing Kelvyn Bell (former guitar player with the band Defunkt) was inspirational for me, and I had a distinct feeling, even though I didn't have a concrete means of achieving it, that whatever I ended up doing with my life, I wanted to make people feel the way this music was making me feel. The only problem was that I wasn't a guitar player and I wasn't a bass player and I wasn't a drummer and I wasn't a singer, I was a dancer and a party maniac, and I didn't quite know how to parlay that into a job.[23]

Keidis's words are particularly interesting because they highlight a dilemma that many people seeking a greater life face. If you are not born with an obvious natural talent but, like Keidis, still have a strong desire to do something out of the ordinary, how do you go about making a name for yourself?

Fortunately, Keidis touches upon the solution in his book. During the summer of 1982, a song was released that had a significant impact on his way of thinking. It was called *The Message*, and as Keidis explains, it opened his mind to the idea that genius can be displayed in many forms:

...more than anything else, *The Message* started to get me thinking. These guys were all writing rhymes, something that Hillel and I had been in love with for a long time. He and I would break into the top floor of the Continental Hyatt House on Sunset, which was a private club, and we'd have it to ourselves and look out at this spectacular view of the city, and we'd smoke a joint and invent these crazy characters and spontaneously erupt into these rhyming sessions. It was the first time I had ever attempted rapping.

So when *The Message* became the hottest thing that summer, it started dawning on me that you don't have to be Al Green or have an incredible Freddie Mercury voice to have a place in the world of music. Rhyming and developing a character were another way to do it.[24]

Here we have Keidis's realisation that it's not necessary to possess genius in The System's sense of the word. He understood that there are ways and means of being great without having an obvious natural talent. What he had to do was express his own unique but less apparent form of genius. It just so happened this lay in his lyrical ability and the development of characters or alter egos. Although not as awe inspiring as a fantastic singing voice, it still offered him a way to make people feel excited about his music.

An example of this unique genius can be seen at the start of his career when, on occasions, Keidis would encourage the band to take to the stage naked with only socks to cover their modesty. Although reflecting nothing of their musical ability, it said something about their attitude, demonstrating a level of boldness in their approach to life. The audience picked up on this and connected with the band's raw energy. This, in turn, helped them connect with the music.

A critic may have called it an attention-grabbing stunt, but Keidis saw the bigger picture when it came to his bands appeal. If they could develop their characters, so that it complimented their music, then they'd create an identity that would distinguish them from other bands. It proved to be an ingenious strategy, as the Red Hot Chilli Peppers went on to have a very successful career spanning multiple decades and selling millions of records.

Keidis's realisation should also help you in your own

quest for greatness. Essentially, it makes the task easier. If it's no longer about untouchable geniuses who were born with outstanding abilities, but finding that particular thing that you do like nobody else, the possibility of greatness now becomes real.

To make sure that you to turn this possibility into a reality, here is a quick checklist on how to be visited by your genius.

1. **Believe that it's possible.** If you see yourself as "ordinary" or lacking the talent necessary to do anything significant then you will never be able to connect with your genius. You won't recognise those flashes of intuition for what they really are. Therefore, it's of the utmost importance that you believe in the potential to be visited by genius. If you need proof, look back over your life to when you had a brilliant idea that turned out to be successful or felt like you were divinely guided while engaged in an exciting activity.

2. **Listen rather than Control.** A deeper awareness of your intuition must be developed. This differs from conscious thought (where you deliberately focus on something). Intuition comes to you in a flash. It isn't deliberate and it can strike at the strangest of times. It usually occurs in moments of mental rest, after you've been concentrating on a particular subject or problem. It might be an idea for a blog post you want to write, a business opportunity you can exploit or a discovery relating to your particular line of work. Because of the irregular nature of these

flashes, it's useful to always have a pen and paper handy, or your phone, so you can record what your genius reveals to you.

3. **Look for heightened emotions.** An accompanying feeling of excitement is usually a great indicator that you have been visited by genius. You may want to bounce up and down or pump your fists or sing and dance. This is a great sign. You feel this way for a reason. Your genius is revealing something that could have a significant impact on your life.

4. **Don't over analyse.** Too much conscious thinking will kill the moment. Don't question it. Either write it down or let it play through you if you are performing. Don't think about how long it will last or whether it will lead to something great; just acknowledge it for what it is. The product, article or business idea it may lead to won't always be a success. Sometimes, there's a failure in execution. Sometimes, this teaches you something that'll make your next product or article even better. So, don't get frustrated if every moment of genius doesn't lead to a greatness. Eventually, one will. Finally, never doubt you'll run out of these moments. They'll always be there so long as you believe they'll come.

Perhaps now you'll understand genius in a new light. Maybe those greats, who we spend our time marvelling at, are just so-called ordinary people with the simple distinction that they know how to connect with, and let in, the intuition of their subconscious mind. Could that be all that separates you from taking your place by their side?

Whatever the case, for you to advance in your own journey, you're going to have to learn how to connect with this power. Hard work, persistence and playing by the rules will only get you so far. To take the next step, and really excel, you have to demonstrate some creativity and flair in whatever you choose to do.

Ultimately, this is what separates those who are trapped in The System from those who break free. There are many intelligent and hardworking people living in The System. However, they are not *creators*.

If you are ever to achieve greatness, this is what you must become. It may not be a ground-breaking invention, or a discovery that cures cancer, but you'll have to leave your original mark on the world. This is the only way that The System's rules can no longer constrain you. By tapping into a power that is greater than The System, *you* begin to set the agenda.

The Invisible Prison

The System imposes vast limits on our freedom. Health destroying working hours, uninspiring schools, heavy taxes, the necessity of making money to survive or support a family and, in some cases, limits on where we can travel. These are just a small sample of the 21st century's restrictions. However, even these can be overshadowed by the limits we place on ourselves.

My job wouldn't be complete if I neglected to address the self-imposed imprisonment that so many of us fall victim to. There can't be true freedom in your life until you release yourself from the grasp of fears, doubts and negative thinking. Not only do these states prevent you from experiencing happiness, they stop you from connecting with your Soul Power, make you hesitate when it's time to advance, influence you to believe you can't succeed and blind you from seeing the bigger picture. For these reasons, it's essential to delve deeper into their destructive impact and present you with a solution.

Imagine a prison. See thick, force field like bars surrounding you in the manner of a cage. Within this cage is the essence of who you are. All your talents, character, unique perspective and personality rolled into a dynamic ball of energy that has the power to bring love, happiness, laughter, knowledge and inspiration into this world. However, every time you give into negative thinking, or are consumed by doubts and fears, your essence gets trapped as the prison bars get stronger.

As a result, the world stops seeing the gifts you have to offer and is, instead, left with a shell of a person only able to function and communicate according to societal norms. This is the impact of negative thinking. Eventually, it will confine you to a reality one tenth of the scope of what it could be. That's why you *must* learn to identify the occasions when fear is ruling your thinking and decision-making process. Furthermore, you must become acutely aware of the times when you doubt your abilities and choices.

To help you with this discovery, read the following list. It details some of our most common fears and negative thoughts. All of them harm your opportunity to realise your potential, enjoy your day to day life and connect with your genius.

- The fear of what other people might think or say.
- The fear of failure.
- Anxiety about what might go wrong in the future.
- The mental attention you give to your illnesses and ailments. (Both mental and physical and psychosomatic and real).
- The mental attention you give to your hang ups (inadequacies about the way you look, dwelling on past failures, comparing yourself negatively to other people).
- Worrying about your ability to perform (speaking, sports, socially, sexually).
- The fear of being isolated and alone.
- The fear of poverty or not having enough money.
- The fear of making the wrong decision and the constant questioning of the decisions you've make.
- The doubt about your work being good enough.

These are the bars of The Invisible Prison. The more time you spend thinking about them, the stronger they become. Of course, momentary consideration is of no concern, but if you find yourself occupied with any, or all of these thoughts, then the consequences will be severe.

I've had my own life restricting experience at the hands of The Invisible Prison. At one stage, every day saw me incarcerated by the hang ups and fears in my mind. A typical day would go like this;

I would wake in the morning, feel the pain in my shoulder from an old rugby injury and spend the next few hours wondering whether it would ever heal. After that, I'd get concerned about my eyes and wonder whether the left one was bloodshot. In any conversation, I wasn't thinking about what the other person was saying but whether they could see my eye.

After lunch, I usually got a bloated sensation in my stomach. Although various doctors said there was nothing wrong, I felt like I needed the toilet but was unable to go. This would then make me worry if I could perform well if I had a football or tennis match that afternoon.

By evening, I was exhausted from a day spent worrying about my hang ups and conditions. However, rather than drifting into a deep sleep, my mind would begin focusing on whether I would get enough rest. I needed my energy for the next day but all I could think about was how terrible it would be if I spent another day feeling so drained.

I was at university at the time, but you wouldn't have known. Thoughts about my studies rarely entered my mind. What were supposed to be the best years of my life passed me by. I couldn't enjoy them because I existed in the world of my problems. What could have been a great time was stolen by The Invisible Prison.

Even once I'd left university, and put these particular issues behind me, my mind still needed a new negative to focus on. Now, it turned its attention to what I should be doing with my life. Should I pursue my dreams or just conform to the wishes of my parents and the path of my peers?

This question bothered me on a daily basis. Mulling it over and over in my mind, I only became more confused. I was repeating the same pattern I got into at university. I was obsessed with finding an answer, yet didn't understand that my constant questioning displayed a lack of faith in my ability to do so.

A few years later, I realised I wasn't the only one who experienced the effects of The Invisible Prison. Hypnotherapy clients would tell me about how they'd tried to stop smoking but all they could think about was having another cigarette. Those wanting to lose weight told spent their whole day thinking about their next meal. The ones with phobias altered their lives so they didn't have an encounter with whatever they feared.

It seemed evidence of The Invisible Prison's influence was everywhere. I looked at teenagers, excessively concerned about what other kids thought of them and noticed its evil grip. I observed adults, too afraid to pursue their dreams for fear of the financial and social ramifications of failure. I even noticed the elderly, with limited time left to enjoy, still preoccupied by money concerns and day to day trivialities. I looked and I saw The Invisible Prison on a grand scale - *a swirling preoccupation with negative thoughts that disconnects us from who we really are and what we're here to do.*

So, how do you break free? Nobody intentionally falls victim to their doubts, fears and negative thinking, but because so few are aware of how their subconscious mind operates, they inevitably get trapped. The best intentions in the world won't help if you approach your freedom as if it's any other obstacle that needs to be overcome. In fact, the most important lesson you could learn is that The Invisible Prison *can't be beaten.*

The Escape

To free yourself from your fears, doubts and negative thinking, you must further develop the ability to let go. The Invisible Prison doesn't operate like its real life equivalent. Rather than using force, you need take a step back from your fear. The more you dwell on your problems, and the more you engage in the negative energy of what you're worried about, the more you get dragged into the vortex of your concerns.

This occurs because of the pink elephant syndrome. Tell yourself not to think about a pink elephant and what happens? In order not to think of one, first you have to think of one. It's an example of your subconscious not being able to process a negative. It only sees what you're thinking about irrespective of whether you have a "don't" "not" or "can't" in front of it. Therefore, all of those occasions when you thought you were fighting a problem (by telling yourself that it had gone away or that you'd beaten it); you were actually maintaining its existence. Your subconscious mind couldn't process the negative and, instead, only registered the issue you're *still* thinking about.

Understanding this phenomenon is the key to breaking free from The Invisible Prison. Most people will try to fight their way out of negative thinking. Unfortunately, this is like thrashing around in quick sand. It only tends to drag you deeper into your problem as *any form of mental attention keeps your issues alive.* You may believe you're freeing yourself from your doubts and fears by saying, "I'm not going to be fat anymore," "I'm not going to fail" or "I'm not going to let my nerves ruin this important occasion," but you're actually doing the reverse. The Invisible Prison's bars are reinforced every time you focus on your troubles.

There's only one solution to escaping an enemy that's kept alive every time you think about it. Like cutting off the oxygen to a flame, you must deny The Invisible Prison the fuel it needs to exist. This involves doing something that doesn't come naturally to most people. Y*ou must rewire your instincts.* Every time you return to fearful thoughts, every time you doubt your chances of success and every time you start dwelling on your issues, you must call on your ability to *let go.*

This is how you free yourself from the quick sand of your own subconscious mind. Don't struggle with your fears, don't try to reason yourself out of them, don't even entertain them. *Just let go.* Refuse to have anything to do with them. **Repeat "LET GO" if it helps**. Do whatever you have to but direct your attention away from the issue. Substitute your fear for *faith.* Tell yourself that whatever it is that's troubling you, will ultimately be resolved.

So, if you're struggling to grow your business, and are constantly thinking about how little progress you've made, *command* your mind to "let go". Then, tell yourself opportunities to increase your sales or gain new clients are heading your way. If you're worried about the future, and live life with a feeling that a disaster in your health, work or relationship is looming, *command* your mind to "let go". Then, tell yourself that everything will be fine and you'll be protected and happy. Finally, if you're overly concerned about your physical appearance, and focus daily on what you feel are your flaws, *command* your mind to "let go". Then, tell yourself that you're happy with your appearance and that you accept the way you look.

This is the key to freedom from negative thinking and also the method by which you positively programme your subconscious mind. It's very difficult to deliberately think of nothing. Instead, discard negative thoughts by telling yourself that whatever needs to happen, (for them to be resolved) will occur. This then activates the power of belief and allows your subconscious to get to work on finding a solution. It will work with, rather than against you, by trusting it to do a job it's more than capable of completing.

Developing this level of faith requires a lot practice. Anybody who has experienced confidence-crippling fears or life restricting hang-ups knows how strong their grip can be. When feeling trapped, so that the mere thought of your issue causes feelings of panic, depression or inadequacy, you have to be incredibly persistent in your attempts to let go. The temptation will always be there to fight or question. This urge *must not be obeyed*. Instead, remember there's nothing forcing you to hold onto negative thoughts. *They don't represent the truth*. They're not part of you. They're just habitual thoughts that have taken residence in your mind. You must separate these thoughts from what you want to achieve.

Free to do Anything

Coming into spiritual awareness meant more than rituals and sacrifices and public prayer. It involved a repentance of a deeper kind; a repentance that was an inner psychological shift based on the suspension of the ego's addictions, and a transcendent "letting go," which would ensure the true fruits of the spiritual life.

- James Redfield, *The Tenth Insight*

One of the many benefits of letting go of your doubts, fears and negative thoughts is the connection it facilitates with the Universe. In an instant, you can go from stressed, drained and worried about the future, to inspired, elated and living in the now. No matter how desperate your situation may seem, letting go has the power to cut through all the negativity. The shackles fall off, the bars are lifted and for as long as you can free your mind from your fears, you get to enjoy this wonderful connection.

Such a powerful experience begs the question, "Why do we allow our fears and hang ups to rule our lives? If we can feel great in the midst of a difficult situation, why do we give our issues such power?"

When you start asking these questions, it's the first sign you're seeing through The System's greatest illusion. It wants you to believe that being miserable and worrying about what might happen are inescapable parts of life.

Perhaps now, though, you realise this isn't the case. As paradoxical as it may seem, you actually choose to be depressed and maintain your hang ups. Not in the sense that you want to live your life this way, but because you give your doubts and fears so much mental attention. If you were to take a step back and realise you have the power to let go of whatever is bothering you, then you'd soon prove to yourself you don't have to remain chained to negativity. In fact, you can be rid of it in an instant and feel so much better. All you need is awareness, discipline and faith in the idea your fears will be resolved.

Having the strength to take this leap of faith will say a lot about your chances of escaping The System. So many people can't cross this threshold because they fear losing control. As a result, the idea that letting go could lead to a greater way of living appears a non-starter. Take your foot off the pedal? Release your need to control? In a system where we're under constant pressure to perform, it appears a recipe for disaster.

However rational a fear of letting go may appear, though, it only represents a surface level understanding of the concept. Glance beyond The System's veil and you'll see it releases you from the restrictive influences in your life. As Tyler Durden says, *"It's only after we've lost everything that we are free to do anything."*

Letting go is about the loss of personal constraints. It's not about losing your possessions, your self-esteem, your friends and security, but the loss of everything that holds you back. The fear of what might happen, the anxiety of being unable to cope, the worry of losing what you already have, the addictions you believe you need and the obsessions that can rule your mind. You can be free from all of these.

With this new insight, you may now realise that any fear of letting go is simply a misunderstanding. You don't have to maintain control all of the time and worry endlessly to make things happen. There is a greater way of living and this will be revealed when you begin to trust in your own genius, rather than struggle to keep up with The System's pace.

Chapter 11
How to Overcome Adversity

Equipped with soul power, transformed by the power of belief and freed from the need to control, you are now ready to seize greatness. You've discovered how The System limits your outlook and realised that by rejecting its conditioning, a new world of opportunity is yours. You no longer think or feel like everybody else. Instead, connected with your inspiration, you are guided towards a genuine reason for living. While others grind away, doing what they're expected to do, your sights are set higher. Freedom and greatness are your hunger, and you won't stop until you're satisfied.

As a result of this transformation, you may now feel ready to take the plunge. Like Neo in *The Matrix*, the wires are about to be torn out and the cords disconnected. You're going to take your first few steps with a free mind, unaccountable to notions of what you *should* be doing.

However, at the same time, you're green. Like a child, you're full of enthusiasm but unsure of what's next. There's a burning question that needs to be answered. What happens when you stop following The System's rules and start living life on your own terms?

Here's what to expect . . .

The Pull of The System

The System exerts an almost magnetic pull. In your decision to break free, you stand alone, isolated and without a path to follow. For the first time in your life, you're going to have to make your own way and following the path of your peers will no longer suffice.

This places you in a precarious position. With no one to guide you, the temptation to return to what you know is strong. This is the pull of The System. No matter how much you want to break free, familiarity provides comfort when faced with adversity. And make no mistake, adversity lies ahead. Your decision to escape The System will be met with a litany of trials and obstacles and, unfortunately for you, they hit hardest at the start.

This adversity strikes on two debilitating levels. Firstly, you'll have to deal and compete with a world where you are now an outsider. Colleagues and friends may distance themselves from you as your decision to pursue greatness exposes the neglect of their own dreams. The System will attempt to influence you into believing your plans for greatness are impossible to achieve. There will be very few sources to guide you because what you're doing is unique and runs counter to conventional wisdom.

Added to this, you're at your weakest point. You haven't yet developed the skills and strengths that come from testing yourself against The System. You don't know how to handle all of the adversity that lines your path. All you have is a faint idea of how you want your life to be and a burning desire to achieve it.

With so many factors working against you, it's no surprise you're going to feel the pull of The System. From the outside, looking in, life can appear much easier when living by The System's rules. You have your job, your group of friends, your position in society and most of the material comforts you require. Why turn your back on this life of relative ease and comfort?

This question may eat away at you during the initial stages of breaking free. It'll make the pursuit of greatness appear an unnecessary burden and, in such moments, the pull of The System can feel overwhelming. You'll tell yourself you can accept second best, that you'll make do and that other people will understand if you were to give up. All of these thoughts will pass through your mind when your quest seems at its most hopeless.

At this point, you'll need something to reaffirm your commitment. Such inspiration is sometimes found in the most unlikely of places. Although the majority of people begrudgingly accept the life The System offers, a few don't. The fictional story of a man who rejected it, provides the perfect metaphor for your current situation.

A Mission Statement for Greatness

The film, *Jerry Maguire*, portrays a man struggling with an early mid-life crisis. At 35, Jerry is a successful sports agent, involved in big money deals and representing some of the world's greatest athletes. However, behind this veneer of success, he's become disillusioned with the industry.

He's detached from the reason *why* he wanted to become a sports agent. Dissatisfied with an entirely commercial approach to his work, he desperately feels the need for change. He's fed up with all the lying and the general insincerity that he and his colleagues bring to the office. He wants to return to the fundamental values (the holistic well-being of the client) on which his company was formed and the change the exploitative nature of the industry.

Jerry puts all of these thoughts down in a moment of inspiration. He stays up all night writing a mission statement which, he hopes, will usher in a new direction for his company. However, although the statement is met with initial enthusiasm, soon the knives are out.

Jerry's mission statement is career suicide. He's fighting the fundamental logic of The System by saying his company's primary concern should not be making money, but the welfare of their clients. As a result, he's fired. What started as a moment of inspiration has left him out on his own and at odds with the world.

You may find yourself in this predicament when initially breaking free from The System. The document Jerry wrote may represent how you feel about your job or life. You may want to live and work for an ideal, rather than just to make money. However, taking such a stand lines your path with adversity.

The Issue of Compromise

When Jerry wrote his mission statement it was a night of inspiration. He was buzzing, the ideas were flowing and he made a connection with his *why*. In the film, it's interesting to hear what he has to say about this experience. He remarks that, "*I'll be the first to admit what I was writing was somewhat touchy feely, but I didn't care. I had lost the ability to bullshit. It was the me I'd always wanted to be!*"[25]

This comment speaks volumes about the force that inspires a person to break free from The System. It's the sense of pride in being true to yourself, it's the relief of not having to bullshit and it's the peace of mind knowing what you're living for is good and right. In short, the prize is that *you no longer have to compromise your identity and conscience.*

This must be remembered, the next time you feel the pull of The System. Although the adversity you face may appear insurmountable, a valuing who you are, and what you stand for, is enough to keep driving you on.

If you need a little extra help, then it's worth remembering the title of Jerry's mission statement, "*The Things we Think and do not Say.*" It explains the conscience and identity denial that occurs when following The System's rules. You could be facing years neglecting your true desires and, ultimately, end up living a lie.

The unappealing prospect of this happening is what made Jerry change. Although he could have kept his head down and continued being successful in his job, there was something inside that wouldn't permit him to rest. It gnawed away at him every time he screwed somebody in a deal. It made him stop to think every time he convinced one of his clients to play on while injured. This voice kept whispering away, telling him that what he was doing was wrong. Eventually, it drove him to the point where he could no longer ignore its call.

Like Jerry, you might hear this voice in your current line of work. Perhaps it wants you to stick with your present job but change the way you operate. Or, perhaps it wants you to use your talents in an entirely different field. In whatever way this voice calls, you'll have to decide whether to heed your conscience or succumb to The System.

If you find yourself without a choice, and simply can't ignore the inspired call of your conscience, then you'll need some extra support. In the initial stages of your quest, when failure is inevitable, it takes something special not to give up. Although drive and will power may eventually see you through, there is a much quicker way to overcome adversity. To find it, you'll have to learn a new skill that requires a different way of understanding your challenges.

Changing the Meaning of Failure

There is no failure only feedback.

– *NLP* Presupposition

The System teaches you to understood failure as an end point. Each time you fail it means one of two things. Either, you lack the talent and skills needed to succeed in that particular field. Or, you're too ambitious in your desires and what you want is not achievable.

Both interpretations validate The System's worldview. They remind you that both you, and the world you live in, are full of limitation. What could be clearer? Your failure is proof.

This understanding of failure can't be accepted, though, if you want to escape The System. In the early stages of your journey, it can damage your morale. On a daily basis you'd be confronted with evidence that The System can't be beaten as you struggle to come to terms with the trial and error process involved in creating a greater life. Each setback will be interpreted as a dead end because you accept the finality that failure represents. It wouldn't be long before you discarded any idea of living a greater life and quietly slipped back into the fold.

The possibility of this occurring is the reason you must develop a new understanding of failure. You have to change its meaning so that it no longer validates your limitations but, instead, becomes a stepping stone to success.

Making this shift takes more than a stretch of the imagination. Currently, you may hate to lose and abhor the way failure seems to delay your progress. It dents your confidence and makes you question whether you've got what it takes to succeed. Failure can easily be interpreted in this way, but before you do, there's an important point you must remember – *The System's truths are based largely upon perception.*

This means you have the freedom to choose. If you don't want failure to mean you haven't got what it takes to succeed, it doesn't have to. It can mean something entirely different. In fact, far from being a disastrous end point, it could mean one of many things. It could become an experience fundamental to your growth. It could be a sign, alerting you to an area of your character or skill base that, once improved, will enable you to advance. You could even tell yourself that the greater the potential for failure, the greater the glory when you succeed.

These are just some of the numerous ways of looking at failure. All of them remove the finality from the experience. Believing in any one of them will help you react differently to your setbacks. Eventually, your understanding of failure will change to a learning experience guiding you to the next level in your life.

A Patent for Success

The effectiveness of this new understanding can't be underestimated. Exactly how it can help you overcome adversity is best demonstrated through an example from the famous inventor, Thomas Edison. He experienced numerous failures while working on his inventions. However, he interpreted them in a way that permitted the continuation of his work.

An example of this can be seen in a well-known anecdote when a journalist asked Edison, who had failed thousands of times while finding a suitable filament for an incandescent light, whether it was now time to give up. Edison replied by saying, "*If I find 10,000 ways something won't work, I haven't failed. I am not discouraged, because every wrong attempt discarded is another step forward.*"

Undoubtedly these comments would have surprised the journalist as they are not the typical attitude one would take to 10,000 failures. Usually this result could only mean one thing - give up. However, Edison clearly had a completely different way of interpreting failure.

Far from meaning an outright defeat, it was simply part of a journey that would end in the discovery of a winning formula. Therefore, failure was not a reason to give up, but something that was leading him to success.

Such an attitude helped Edison on his way to becoming one of history's most prolific inventors. With 1,098 U.S patents to his name, his example stands as a testament to the power of changing the meaning of failure.

In doing so, it also carries important implications for your life. Maybe you've quit too easily in the past or are allowing the prospect of failure to prevent you from escaping The System and pursuing your dreams. If this is the case then you must find a way to change the meaning of failure. Perhaps you'll follow Edison's lead and use it as an experience that alerts you to an incorrect approach. Or, perhaps you'll use the memory of your defeats as motivation to drive you on. Whatever meaning you choose to attach, you must change your understanding of the experience in a way that *permits the continuation of your journey.*

Ready For Anything

Being "ready for anything" is about developing fearlessness when confronting adversity. You must be brave to the end when facing the initial loss of finance, security and status that breaking free from The System can sometimes bring.

After all, half the adversity you face is psychological. The fear of failure can be even more powerful than the event itself. In extreme cases, it could cause you to shy away from challenges fundamental to your growth. That's why it's so important to be ready for anything. It's only by adopting this mentality that you'll have the strength to test yourself day after day.

A good example of this can be found in the best-selling book, *The Game*. In this real-life story, Neil Strauss (the author), uses this mentality to transform himself from dateless desperado to master pick up artist.

Strauss is a journalist with non-existent love life. Despite being in his thirties, he has had few relationships and frequently faces rejection whenever he makes an approach. He feels time is running out and, in an attempt, to salvage his love life, he contacts the self-proclaimed "world's greatest pick up artist."

This proves to be a life changing moment. The man he meets is Mystery, an eccentric who has spent years studying and practising the art of picking up girls. He teaches Strauss all he knows and one of his most important lessons is about being prepared for failure.

"My job here is to get you into the game," he continues, making piercing eye contact with each of us. "I need to get what's in my head into yours. Think of tonight as a video game. It is not real. Every time you do an approach, you are playing this game."

My heart began pounding violently. The thought of trying to start a conversation with a woman I didn't know petrified me, especially with these guys watching and judging me. Bungee jumping and parachuting were a cakewalk compared to this.

"All your emotions are going to try to fuck you up," Mystery continued. "They are there to try to confuse you, so know right now that they can-not be trusted at all. You will feel shy sometimes, and self-conscious, and you must deal with it like you deal with a pebble in your shoe. It's uncomfortable, but you ignore it. It's not part of the equation." . .

"I need to teach you, in four days, the whole equation – the sequence of moves you need to win." Mystery went on. "And you will have to play this game over and over to win. So get ready to fail."[26]

Mystery's advice helped Strauss to become one of the greatest pick up artists in their community. Over the course of a year he underwent a rapid transformation in his appearance, confidence levels and social skills. He even adopted a new name – Style - to reflect this new persona.

As Style, was able to pick up a different woman every night and was seducing girls that wouldn't have looked twice prior to his transformation. All of this was possible because of his *readiness to fail.*

It was this attitude that enabled him to keep plugging away. Night after night, he would be in nightclubs approaching women. It didn't matter if some turned him down because he realised this was all part of the process. Therefore, he worked on the areas that needed improving, asked questions, sought advice and got straight back in the game. It was as if the failures didn't register. His mind was focused on something greater and because of this focus; he didn't interpret his setbacks as reasons to give up.

Such a transformation has important implications for you. Mystery makes many useful points. In particular, the comments about treating the task of picking up women as a "video game" are priceless. This trick takes the edge off any nerve raking experience. By desensitising the meaning of what you're doing, you create a shift in perception that distances your emotions from what is happening. This enables you to hone whatever skills you need without the detrimental impact associated with failure. After all, if you're just playing a game, and not facing judgement on your worth, then why should failure matter?

Mystery also wanted Strauss to understand the journey to becoming a pick-up artist. He knew Strauss's emotions and instincts would, initially, be working against him. Furthermore, he knew Strauss would experience situations where words would elude him and that he might embarrass himself while making an approach. However, he also knew this was only temporary and an important part of Strauss's overall growth.

This is why he wanted Strauss to adopt a blasé attitude to any setbacks he experienced. He realised the vital role that failure played in teaching his students the right and wrong way to becoming master pick up artists.

An appreciation for the nature of the journey to greatness will also help *you* gain a sense of perspective when experiencing failure. On your way to the top, you can expect breakthroughs, consolidation periods and then moments of despair. You may feel on top of the world for a month but then, a week later, find yourself questioning where it all went wrong. Throughout these ups and downs, if you can realise this is all part of the process and that each failure is just leading to your eventual success, then progress is assured. So, get ready to fail and realise that by doing so, you gain unlimited opportunities to develop the knowledge needed to succeed.

You Can't Fail

Once you've faced enough challenges your "ready for anything" mentality will evolve into something stronger. A transition will occur and you'll begin to believe *you can't fail*.

This transition marks an important stage in your journey. It signifies a milestone in your understanding and a shift away from the finality of failure. It's not that you won't ever fail again. It's just that you'll interpret these failures differently. You'll be able to *detach outcome from mentality* and realise that you only truly fail when you accept defeat in your mind.

As a result, your capacity to be negatively affected by your setbacks will diminish. You'll realise that over a long enough timeframe, given the strategies you are now adopting, success is inevitable.

With such a realisation comes a supreme level of confidence. Ask yourself this question, "If there was no possibility of failure, what would I do with my life?" With a "can't fail" mentality you can now live out the answer. All it takes is the belief you can turn every outcome to your advantage.

Vince Lombardi, two-time Super Bowl winning head coach epitomised this mentality. He summarised it perfectly with a one sentence response when questioned by a journalist after one of his teams' rare defeats, "*We didn't lose the game; we just ran out of time.*"

This comment represents a "can't fail" mentality. It's the refusal to accept that you can be beaten. He may have said it with a sense of irony but the implication was clear – *defeat doesn't register*. Even when the score line is against you, maintain unshakable belief in yourself.

This attitude sets a benchmark for any person pursuing a greater life. It demonstrates a level of boldness that you should strive to emulate when combating adversity. It also enables you to do something that could be described as the hallmark of greatness - *perform without the fear of failure.* For if you truly believe you can't fail, concern about the outcome is removed from the equation. No matter what approach you take, or path you follow, success is assured.

Examples of this ability to perform without the fear of failure can be seen with all the great teams and individual performers of our time. Observe a World Cup winning Brazilian football team moving the ball around the pitch. Watch Roger Federer play in a championship final or Michael Jackson perform in concert. They all do what they do without concern for what might go wrong. As a result, when performing, they are able to give the best of themselves. While many people would be terrified at the consequences of high stakes failure, they're so certain of themselves, the fear barely registers.

Such strength of belief is vital as your journey continues. The pull of The System may have been hard to resist but there's more adversity lying ahead. To take the final steps, you're going to have to overcome the odds and face a deck stacked firmly against you.

Chapter 12
How to Grow Stronger than The System

Far better it is to dare mighty things, to win glorious triumphs even though chequered by failure, than to rank with those poor spirits who neither enjoy nor suffer much because they live in the grey twilight that knows neither victory nor defeat.

- Theodore Roosevelt

Before you can progress any further, you must understand the implications of your decision to escape The System. By choosing this path, you place yourself on the fringe, rejecting the commonly held beliefs about the way the world works. Added to this, you have your sights set on a greater prize. You dream about how life could be and refuse to let The System condition you into believing it's unachievable.

As a result of this defiance, adversity is inevitable. *Escaping The System is about breaking down barriers* and, in doing so, you're bringing a burden upon yourself that most people can avoid. Your peers, your friends and your family won't have to put themselves on the line like you do. They can avoid many hardships because they don't challenge the way the world works. However, you do, and when your ambition knows no boundaries, a battle with The System becomes unavoidable.

When preparing for this battle, you must realise The System doesn't surrender easily. In your pursuit of greatness, you challenge its legitimacy and threaten to expose the illusion of its authority. As a result, it will line your path with every obstacle imaginable.

To start with, *your best won't be good enough*. You have to set higher standards than the person who plays by The System's rules. They can survive by working hard, obeying orders and copying other people. You, on the other hand, have a double battle to fight. Not only do you have to stay afloat, you must also break new ground.

This means going the extra mile. When a colleague of clocks off at five, six or seven pm, you might have to put in an extra hour and a half's work on your new business idea. While their work only has to impress their boss or a client; yours must be good enough to build an audience from across the world. And while they might only have to learn, reproduce and follow a formula, you might have to create something from scratch.

Doing "good enough" won't cut it and the constant

pressure to excel is demanding. On a daily basis, you'll have to squeeze the most out of yourself and display a super human commitment to your cause. Anything less, and The System's mediocrity net will ensure you remain trapped.

On top of this, you have to overcome the psychological warfare The System uses to keep people down. This is likely to operate through the media and, sadly, the people who know you best. Work colleagues, school teachers, careers advisors, friends and family, all influenced by The System, will sow the seeds of doubt in your mind. They'll imply that what you want to achieve isn't possible and interpret every failure as evidence it's time to give up. This psychological onslaught can have severe consequences. If accepted, it can easily knock your confidence and cause you to question whether a life free from The System could ever exist.

With these doubts floating around, it's not a good time to be short of money. You're following your inspiration (not The System's logic of making money at all costs) and, in the short term, this could place you in a difficult position. You might have to leave your present job, venture out on your own, start a new business or pursue an artistic or creative goal that will not pay you for many years to come. Can you handle the initial sacrifice this might entail? Can you cope with the prospect of not having as much money as you used to? Can you deal with your peers climbing ahead on the financial ladder while you toil away at what might seem like an unrealistic dream?

All of these questions can eat away at you and make the decision to turn your back on The System seem crazy. You'll feel this sting even more acutely if you buy into The

System's credo that the more you have, and the more you own, the happier you will be. If this is the case, then you're facing the prospect of an almost daily battle with the thought of what you're giving up.

This wall of adversity is only half the equation though. There's more to come and if you continue to break down the barriers then The System will uneven the playing field. It'll lie, it'll cheat and it'll play dirty. The System will use every tactic imaginable to prevent you from exposing the illusion of its authority.

If it doesn't want you to advance then it can *manipulate the law* (Rubin "Hurricane" Carter being falsely imprisoned for murder as he was emerging as a politically outspoken boxer with world championship credentials in 60's America), *deny all reason and scientific evidence* (Galileo's theories about the earth rotating around the sun or the initial denial of climate change) and *discredit your reputation* (the media working to marginalise people or groups presenting a point of view that veers away from the mainstream). It can and *will* take all of these measures if what you're doing in any way threatens its legitimacy.

This leaves you in a precarious position. Answer your call to greatness and risk adversity. Or, reject your call and deny yourself the opportunity to be great. It's a tough choice and in making this decision you have to think long and hard about who you really are.

In the end, you may decide it's simply not worth it. Few are cut out for the daily struggle of breaking free from The System. However, one thing you're not permitted to do is *make this decision on the grounds of possibility*.

To claim it's impossible to break free from The System

is *not* a valid excuse. History provides examples of thousands of people who've introduced industry disrupting new technology and ideas, changed unjust laws and achieved feats that were considered beyond the capabilities of the human body. Many have walked the path before you and many will continue to do so. Some of them have had the deck so firmly stacked against them that nobody would have blamed them for giving up.

One such man is Carl Brashear. The next section is dedicated to his inspirational story. Read on to discover how he overcame the odds and made The System change.

A Man of Honour

Carl Brashear wanted what he was not supposed to have. In pre-civil rights era America, his dream was to become a Master Diver in the U.S. Navy. At the time (1940s and 50s) this was unheard of. No African American had ever achieved this rank and, in a Navy that was still heavily segregated, the most he could hope for was to be a cook, steward or valet.

For Carl, though, this was unacceptable. Since child-hood he'd dreamed of diving and all of the adventure that goes with a life at sea. This dream had inspired him to leave his father's farm and pursue his destiny by enlisting with the Navy. He didn't join to wash dishes, and while many of his peers begrudgingly accepted the role they were given, Carl refused to compromise. As a result, he faced the full might of The System in his attempts to achieve a goal that, for many, was considered impossible.

Carl's story is popularised in the film, *Men of Honour*.

Through this visual representation of his life, the audience gain an appreciation of the seemingly insurmountable adversity he had to face. Carl contends with racism, lack of education, death threats and the sabotage of his work by colleagues and officers. He has a mountain to climb, and each new trial provides the audience with an insight into just how demanding challenging The System can be.

This is only part of the story, though, as half way through the film Carl is involved in a tragic accident that leaves him disabled. At this stage, he's become a Navy Diver but hasn't realised his full dream of achieving Master Diver status. Such a devastating event appears to put an end to this plan. He's left in a hospital bed, seemingly crippled, with the prospect of a life spent hobbling around on a walking stick ahead.

What happens next is a testament to man's ability to overcome adversity. In a bold move, Carl decides to have his useless leg amputated and re train with a prosthesis. Now, not only does he have to pass a rigorous exam that's too demanding for most able-bodied men, he also has to overcome a new form of discrimination on the grounds of his disability.

Carl's story comes to a head in a final court room scene when he's given the challenge of walking 12 steps in the new navy issue 290-pound diving suit. The naval establishment set him this challenge because they want to see him fail. They view him as a threat. He's already broken-down barriers by becoming the first African American to achieve the rank of Navy Diver (outside war time). They don't want him to continue this trend by being the first to achieve Master Diver status.

For them, the whole idea is an outrage. African Americans are not supposed to be divers, let alone master divers with only one functioning leg. However, no matter what obstacle they place in front of Carl, he always seems to find a way of overcoming their prejudice.

Even in the courtroom, under immense pressure, he is able to walk the 12 steps. With the Navy's final barrier broken, they have no choice but to reinstate and allow him to train towards becoming a Master Diver.

Carl Brashear went on to achieve this rank. He then continued to serve in the Navy for a further ten years finally retiring from active service in 1979. By the time of his retirement, he was already highly decorated, but perhaps his greatest honour came in the year 2000 when he was awarded the Secretary of Defence Medal for 42 years of Outstanding Public Service.

This award put the stamp of greatness on the life of an incredible man. His story stands as a solace giving example for when you face adversity in your own quest. He challenged The System and won. Even though it threw everything at him, unlevelled the playing field, made his dreams appear impossible and threatened him with the loss of his life, he still came through.

In your quest for a greater life you will have your own challenges, but you can always take strength from those that have already walked the path. In particular, you might take some advice from Carl. When interviewed for the film, he talks about his life and discusses his approach to overcoming adversity. He makes an important comment when saying, "*I knew who I was and I knew where I wanted to go. My goals were set and I was going to work towards those goals with all my might and no note* [referring to the death threats he received] *was going to stop me.*"[27]

These words give an insight into what it takes to escape The System. Some of the qualities needed are self-knowledge, a clear idea of where you want to go and a cast iron determination in getting there. If you can develop these qualities then you'll create a mental wall that shields you from adversity. You may even get to the point where it no longer registers. You are *that focused* and determined, you develop a form of tunnel vision that keeps driving you on.

Carl certainly seemed to have found this place. In the interview, he's so self-assured it's difficult to imagine the adversity he faced having any effect on him. This was his secret. If he'd given his adversity any mental attention, he'd have been unable to take the steps needed to become a Master Diver. He'd have started questioning whether he could really do it and the doubts in his mind would have sabotaged his attempts.

This is why it's so important to learn from his example. All the different obstacles you'll have to face, stacked one on top of the other, can seem far too daunting to overcome. Therefore, you need a new way of processing adversity. Remaining focused on your dream, so that you bypass the enormity of the obstacles you face, prevents you from becoming overwhelmed by the scale of your challenge.

Answering the Call

Carl Brashear's story doesn't just demonstrate the attitude you need to overcome adversity; it shines a light on *why* you must be willing to face it. This can be seen mid-way through the film when he's having an argument with his girlfriend, Jo. She wants a quiet life and has no intention of rocking the boat. Carl, on the other hand, has a burning desire for greatness and their differences come to a head after Carl is involved in a bar room confrontation.

Jo: *Don't you see? I'm not like you. The things I want are smaller. If I just work hard and keep my head down.*
Carl: *Your whole life will pass you by.*[28]

With these two lines, we see the necessity of breaking free from The System. Although this path exposes you to adversity, conformity presents its own form of hardship. Carl hints at what lies in store when he says, "*Your whole life will pass you by.*" This is his warning for those who accept The System's path. While challenges to their character and courting the potential for disaster can be avoided, the likelihood of a slow and silent decline is almost undeniable.

This must be remembered if you're ever questioning your decision to escape The System. Knowing that both paths are lined with adversity means you have to look to the potential reward of each route. At best, all The System offers is comfort and security. It can't fill you with a sense of energy and purpose. It can't reward you with the realisation of your dreams. These prizes are exclusive. They remain in the domain of men like Carl Brashear. It's worth remembering this when your climb gets steep. Nothing compares to having the odds stacked against you and winning.

The Stepping Stones to Greatness

Knowing why you're willing to face adversity is one thing. Knowing *how* you're going to overcome it is another. If you have not already escaped The System then there is a transition to make. It's unlikely you'll cruise straight to the top. There is a process by which you grow stronger and gain new skills and it begins with a deeper understanding of adversity. You have to realise that we experience obstacles precisely because *there is something we lack*. Adversity brings these areas to light and for this reason, it must be embraced. It may seem paradoxical, but doing the very thing that makes you tremble with fear, or leaves you feeling unable to cope, is actually *a means to growth*.

With this new understanding, the adversity you face gets turned on its head. No longer a trial you either avoid or begrudgingly accept, it becomes an opportunity to enhance your skills.

The Comfort Zone

To develop the strength and skills to escape The System you must continually break yourself down and build yourself up. Nothing facilitates this process quite like *leaving your comfort zone*. It's this willingness to do the things that make you feel uncomfortable, or out of your depth, that forces you to adapt. When out of your comfort zone, you *have* to learn new skills because you can't survive with the ones you've got. As a result, you rebuild yourself with the attributes you need to continue your climb.

Reading these lines may send a shiver down your spine.

The prospect of deliberately leaving your comfort zone might present a threat to your ego and expose your perceived limitations. You may have worked hard to get yourself into a comfortable place where you don't have to face constant challenges. Why would you want to leave and deliberately put yourself in the firing line?

Although it may be hard to give up the comfort of what you know, it's a step you're going to have to take. You can only maintain while in the comfort zone. For you to move forwards, something has to change. You must remove old blocks and fears and bring to the fore attributes that may have lain dormant for years. This process can only be facilitated by shocking your system. It might be unpleasant, but every time you test your present limitations, you grant yourself the opportunity to improve some aspect of your character or abilities.

Of course, there's a practical element that needs consideration. If your aim is to create a successful blog then you'll want to find mentors who can instruct in both the writing, and selling, of your content. You might also want to subscribe to a digital marketing website so you can learn how to promote yourself. You'll likely need to put in thousands of hours of writing until you become one of the best in your niche. On top of that, you might attend conventions and support groups to become fully immersed in the blogging world.

All of these steps will help you build the skills needed to create a greater life. However, they will be useless if you're not brave enough to continually break the boundaries of your comfort zone.

There'll come a time when your blog has to go live and

you lay your much-loved work open to the criticism of the world. You might also have to contact publishers and agents (when looking to reach a wider audience) and face the daunting prospect of justifying your worth and explaining why it is the world needs to hear your stories. These moments will both strengthen your character and give you new insights into what it takes to succeed in your field. This is how you grow. When both skills and knowledge, and a willingness to do that which makes you feel uncomfortable, are combined, the rate at which you'll advance will rapidly increase.

The following example tells the story of a hypnotherapy client of mine. I include it because of its relevance to the process, and benefits, of breaking free from your comfort zone.

Paul came to see me for help building his confidence at work. He'd been stuck in the same job, without promotion, for over 5 years. He was working in the marketing department and was sure that his career inertia was caused by a fear of speaking up and presenting his ideas.

His goal, he told me, was to become head of the creative team within the next year. He had a firm belief in his ability and a lot of ideas waiting to be put into practice. He also felt he would make an exciting leader but, so far, in spite of all these qualities, had failed to claim the position.

This, he put down to a lack of confidence when it came to expressing his ideas. In every other aspect of his job he believed in his ability. However, when it came to voicing his ideas, he was dumbstruck.

He would panic, forget what he intended to say and be

unable to make eye contact when addressing a group. He described the experience as an emotional high jacking. It felt like someone else was taking over and sabotaging his attempt to communicate all the points he'd planned to make.

As Paul explained his story to me, it became clear that his fear was deeply entrenched. It related back to his childhood where his parents raised him to be obedient and do as he was told. Answering back or any loud behaviour was met with immediate punishment. As a result, he'd grown into an introverted who found it extremely difficult to voice any opinions.

Paul was hoping a few of my techniques would work their magic, requiring little effort on his behalf. However, our sessions didn't go to plan.

I tried all the confidence boosting and regression techniques I knew but Paul only reported minor improvements. Now, he could outline one of his ideas to a colleague but still felt completely unable to take the lead in a group situation.

This left us at a dead end. My interventions weren't working and I was running out of ideas. Added to this, Paul was running out of faith and I knew I would have to do something drastic to get him back on track.

Fortunately, at this point, I remembered a magazine article I'd read while training. It was written by a therapist who was commenting on the limitations of "talking therapies." He felt that clients who showed little response to standard techniques should challenge their limitations by deliberately breaking free from their comfort zone. Repeatedly doing so, he claimed, would put them in a situation where they were *forced to adapt.*

I was very interested in this theory and presented it to Paul as an alternative. He too seemed keen and was ready to proceed. However, in order for this to work, I realised we'd have to change the meaning of what he was about to undertake.

To do this, I induced a trance and suggested that leaving his comfort zone was a means to his professional advance. Furthermore, I suggested that any feelings of panic he might experience were to be interpreted as signals he was on the right track and moving his life forwards. They may make him feel uncomfortable, but they were *to be understood as growing pains* and, therefore, positive.

With this new understanding, I felt Paul would see through his commitment to leave his comfort zone at least once every day. To make sure, we started with something simple. Rather than jump straight into presenting his ideas in a meeting (where he felt at his most vulnerable), Paul thought it would be better to contact his boss directly. This way he could talk to him about his ideas, without the rest of the team being present, and discuss the possibility of chairing a future meeting.

Although not as great a breach of his comfort zone as speaking out in a meeting, the prospect of doing this still made him feel nervous. This was a good thing. It indicated potential for growth. Therefore, we fixed a date for him to contact his boss and Paul left my office to prepare his ideas.

Paul spent a considerable amount of time working on his plans for the upcoming marketing campaign. However, when the day came to speak to his boss, he experienced a powerful attack of nerves.

While walking to work, every feeling in his body was telling him to avoid making the all-important phone call. He kept creating excuses for why it wasn't the right time and told himself he would try again when feeling more confident.

This internal dialogue continued while at work. One part of him wanted to advance; another sought the safety of familiarity. With time running out it seemed the latter impulse would have its way.

At this point, he bumped into a colleague who had recently been promoted. He watched her go about her work and couldn't escape the thought he could do a better job. This grated at Paul and sparked him into action. Shaking with nerves, he called his boss and asked if they could meet. To Paul's surprise, he agreed and they fixed a time for the following day.

If Paul thought this one phone call would be the end of his fears, he was greatly mistaken. He didn't sleep that night, worrying about what he was going to say. As the hours passed, he even contemplated cancelling the meeting. He never thought that leaving his comfort zone could be so hard.

Despite these fears, Paul forced himself into his boss's office. Repeating my words, he reminded himself that the nerves were just part of the growing process. He was changing and this was his bodies' way of adapting to something new.

While his nerves were present throughout the meeting, it was still a success. His boss liked his ideas and agreed to let Paul present them. This was a great achievement for Paul. It marked the first occasion he was able to communicate an idea for a marketing campaign that was uniquely his own.

Of course, when the time came to present in front of the group he was still filled with panic. His gut churned and he felt uncomfortable throughout. However, he drove himself on.

He made sure he finished every hand quivering sentence and sweat inducing section. It was almost unbearable but he kept telling himself that it was making him stronger. Eventually it was done. He'd presented his *own* campaign in front of a group of people and given himself a voice.

Paul and I continued our sessions for a month after this breakthrough meeting. He then sent me a few emails over the next year and a half. I was delighted to find they reported progress. He told me about his surprise at how difficult he found it to break free from his comfort zone. In total, it took him a full year before he really adjusted. Even now, there were occasional moments when he wanted to stay quiet and remain hidden in the background. The easy option still hadn't lost its appeal.

However, despite the awkward moments, Paul felt the practise of deliberately leaving his comfort zone had been worthwhile. In fact, he went so far as to say he felt like a new person.

Self-Crucifixion

Paul's journey was by no means easy. It caused him sleepless nights, immense discomfort and moments of soul-searching confusion. Such an ordeal stands as a testament to the power of the comfort zone.

On one side, you have your mind rationalising the necessity of taking certain steps to achieve your goals. Yet, on the other, your body fires off every unpleasant emotion in an attempt to force you to stick with what you know. The battle that ensues can often feel like you're fighting against your nature.

James Allen, author of *As a Man Thinketh*, describes this experience as "self-crucifixion." He believed those seeking a greater life must go through a process where they destroy the parts of their character preventing them from fulfilling their potential. This is achieved through a willingness to repeatedly face your fears. By doing this, the weaker elements of your character are brought to light, forced to adapt and change. As Allen said:

> Men are anxious to improve their circumstances, but are unwilling to improve themselves; they therefore remain bound. The man who does not shrink from self – crucifixion can never fail to accomplish the object upon which his heart is set. This is as true of earthly as of heavenly things. Even the man whose sole objective is to acquire wealth must be prepared to make great personal sacrifices before he can accomplish his object; and how much more so he who would achieve a strong and well-poised life?[29]

From this quote, and Paul's example, it's clear to see that breaking free from your comfort zone can be a demanding ordeal. As Allen says, it involves, "*great personal sacrifices.*" However, the rewards are even greater.

Allen reminds us that, "The man who does not shrink

from self – crucifixion can never fail to accomplish the object upon which his heart is set." It's a guarantee that if you continually face up to what you are afraid of, you will grow stronger. In turn, this newfound strength will enable you to achieve what you previously couldn't.

To facilitate this change, you have to be deliberate in your commitment to break free from your comfort zone. Rather than being a rare occurrence that happens only at a job interview or when making a romantic approach, leaving this space has to become a daily practice. Every opportunity must be taken.

This is the quickest way to ensure your development. Following this practice will get you to the point where you're equipped with the necessary strengths and skills to escape The System. However, enough emphasis can't be placed on just how deliberate you must be.

Consider The System's influence and you'll understand why this is so important. Every day, it presents you with the easy option. Just do enough to survive and get by. Make sure you earn a living and have a family. This is enough to pass the test.

As a result, it can seem unnecessarily challenging to work on hang ups and insecurities. What's the point? It's possible to survive in The System without doing so. All you have to do is mask them, or avoid situations that might bring them to the fore, and you can continue the pretence of a satisfied life. No one will challenge you because they'd court the possibility of their own façade being exposed.

As someone seeking a greater life, this places you in an awkward position. It means you must become your own motivator. Nobody else will do it for you, and without any external pressure, the easy option becomes even more appealing. However, you'll have to resist.

Others may question why you seem hell bent on making life as difficult as possible, but what they don't realise is you need to develop the strength to live independently of The System. This can only be done by confronting all of your fears. One by one they have to be "crucified." Only then, once the dust has settled, can the greatest version of yourself emerge.

The Pain Barrier

I firmly believe that any man's finest hour, the greatest fulfilment of all that he holds dear, is that moment when he has worked his heart out in a good cause and lies exhausted on the field of battle – victorious.

- Vince Lombardi

The pain barrier, like the comfort zone, is another threshold that must be crossed to develop the strengths and skills needed to escape The System. Typically, it's associated with athletes, especially long-distance runners.

While running, they reach a stage where fatigue sets in and they hit the limit of their endurance. At this point, signals are sent to their brain, telling them to stop. The athlete then has to decide whether they're going to slow down or forge ahead. Those that cross this barrier report finding hidden resources making all the difference to their chances of victory.

In the context of your quest for a greater life, crossing the pain barrier can be applied to all areas of achievement. It could be the physical barrier of demanding more from your body when you want to rest. It could be the emotional barrier of confronting the heartache and loneliness that's, sometimes, associated with forging your own path. Or, it could be the mental barrier of concentrating, and staying focused, when your mind is tempted to wander. Whatever the case, there will be a daily opportunity to push through your pain barrier and, therefore, speed up the rate at which you grow.

For me, the pain barrier presented itself in the form of focused concentration over long periods of time. Countless times I would sit down to write and find that the weaker part of me would want to browse the internet or watch sports clips on YouTube. However, I had to deny this urge to rest, even when it felt like a chore to write, knowing that my concentration and enjoyment of the writing process would increase the more I pushed through.

Then, once the book was complete (this was before I published it – the book you're reading now has been rewritten five times!), I had to deal with the emotional pain barrier of realising it wasn't good enough. I had to suck up the heartache, sit down at my desk, and start making corrections.

It was painful because I thought the book was ready. I didn't want to postpone the release date yet again. However, I had to push through to ensure it was as good as I knew it could be.

Whatever the demands of your quest, there'll be times when you will feel like giving up. These moments occur when you're faced with an obstacle that seems to demand more effort and ability than you think you possess. At this point, you'll confront your pain barrier.

To break through, you'll need more than grit and

determination. It requires a new understanding of your supposed limitations. You'll have to reject The System's view, which encourages us to see ourselves as weak and limited. Then, you must embrace a new outlook, more accepting of the idea you have limitless potential.

Without taking this step, the pain barrier will always be a symbol of validation for The System. It's there to remind you that you can only go so far. There are goals you *can't* achieve. It's the ultimate proof of your limitation.

Fortunately, though, you have a choice as to how you interpret the pain barrier. There's another school of thought that sees this obstacle as less of a wall, *and more of a divide.*

Arnold Schwarzenegger believed in this idea. He had first-hand experience of battling with his pain barrier on a regular basis. Every day in the gym he had to demand more out of his body. To become the greatest bodybuilder on the planet, he had to make it grow. As a result, he subjected himself to progressively harder training routines in order to stimulate his muscles. This meant regularly pushing beyond what his body was used to, and in the process, breaking through his pain barrier.

Such an experience gave him a great insight into what lay beyond the divide. He credits this daily physical and mental practice as the main reason he became a champion. He shares this insight in an interview during the film, *Pumping Iron.*

The body isn't used to the 9th, 10th, 11th 12th rep with a certain weight. So that makes the body grow, going through this pain barrier, experiencing pain in your muscles, aching, and then just going on and on and on. These last 2 or 3 repetitions makes the muscles grow.

That divides one from being a champion and one from not being a champion. If you can go through this pain barrier, you make it to be a champion, if you can't go through, forget it. And that's what most people lack, having the guts to go in and say, "I'll go through the pain barrier and I don't care what happens."

I have no fear of fainting in the gym because I know it could happen. I threw up many times when I was working out but it doesn't matter because it's all worth it.[30]

Arnold's comments reveal a lot about the transformation that occurs when regularly crossing your pain barrier. In fact, the journey a bodybuilder undergoes has many similarities to the one you are undertaking. The key word in both cases is *growth*. Bodybuilding focuses mainly on the physical. The quest for greatness, the metaphysical. However, the process by which this growth occurs shares many similarities.

As Arnold notes, it's the final 2 to 3 repetitions that really hurt. His body has reached its limit, it can take no more, yet he still squeezes them out. As a result, his muscles have been pushed beyond what they are used to and are forced to adapt.

This process can be applied to your quest for greatness. *It's about testing yourself beyond your current capacity.* Whether this is through an extra mile on your weekly run, an extra hour's research into your new business when you return from work, or ten extra phone calls in an attempt to generate more sales, the key is to gradually push beyond what you are used to.

At this point, you'll confront your pain barrier. Your brain will send out signals of emotional, physical or mental distress. Your immediate reaction might be to quit. It hurts and the slump in your energy makes you feel like you can't go on. However, now you realise these feelings aren't a clash with your limitations *but the pain of growth*; you can continue.

In fact, you must face the obstacles that appear to demand more effort and ability than you think you possess because they make you stretch. Like a muscle forced to grow through the demand of a heavier weight, your spirit, emotional endurance and mental stamina will increase as a result of this test.

Then, like the bodybuilder who transforms himself in weight and appearance, you will also appear changed. You'll no longer be that person who believes there's a limit upon their ability. Instead, you'll be someone who realises that if they continually test their limits, then they can go further than they ever thought possible.

Arnold's interview also hints at another significant change that occurs by crossing your pain barrier. You overcome the fear of being challenged. In the interview, he remarks that, "*I'll go through the pain barrier and I don't care what happens.*" The prospect of fainting or throwing up in the gym is of no concern. He knows why he is willing to face the daily struggle of training and this gives his pain meaning.

This is a great place to be because it reflects a mentality that isn't focused on the negatives. As Arnold says, all of the pain "*doesn't matter*" and ultimately, it's "*worth it.*" He is able to say this because he knows these sacrifices are leading to success.

Such comments reveal an important insight into the mind of a man who knows what lies on the other side of the pain barrier. He overcomes adversity knowing the pain he experiences will be washed away by the reward of standing victorious on the winners' podium. This is the best attitude when striving to achieve the next level in any endeavour. Get consumed by the thought of your ultimate success and you numb the pain experienced as a part of your growth.

Bearing the Scars

There are many similarities between crossing the pain barrier and breaking free from the comfort zone. Both involve facing hardship and dealing with unpleasant emotions. However, perhaps the greatest likeness can be found in the way they *harden a person.*

Naïve dreamer to unconquerable believer is the transition you'll make if you persist in the practice of breaking free from your comfort zone and crossing the pain barrier. In the process, you'll get to experience an unglamorous yet completely essential part of achieving greatness. At times you may wish for shortcuts, or pray that your journey gets easier, but there is method to this madness. Ultimately, all of the sacrifices you've made will lead you to a psychological breakthrough as you realise that *adversity is the stepping stone to success.*

The importance of this breakthrough can't be underestimated. Previously, the adversity you've faced may have seemed daunting, if not completely overwhelming. It's so easy, when confronted with yet another obstacle, to give into The System's conditioning and think, "Oh shit, I can't possibly do this!" However, a person who has been hardened by breaking their pain barrier and comfort zone thinks differently.

They no longer see an insurmountable obstacle. Instead, they subconsciously search for ways and means of tackling the problems they face. Their mind has been reprogrammed. The knee jerk reaction of fleeing in the face of adversity has gone. In its place is a belief that, no matter what they face, ultimately, they will succeed.

Achieving this psychological breakthrough is the raison d'etre for continually crossing your pain barrier and breaking free from your comfort zone. Once it has been accomplished most of the fear attached to adversity begins to subside. In its place is a simple understanding of the *process*. You put yourself out there, you get broken down, and then you reform stronger than before.

Adversity: Gift or Curse?

That episode with Ma Beck shook me out of my depression. It started me on my way. After that I told myself that I must do what my mom would have expected me to do. And so, the two greatest tragedies in my life – losing my brother and then my mom – were, strangely enough, extraordinarily positive for me. What I've accomplished since then, really grows out of my coming to terms with those events.

- Ray Charles

Ray Charles was seven when his brother died. Soon after, possibly as a result of the trauma he experienced, he began to lose his sight. Then, at 15, his mother died. She'd been his strength and support, guiding him while he adjusted to a world with no vision.

Perhaps these two events should have finished him. It wouldn't have taken much imagination to see him as a homeless blind man, begging for a living on the streets. However, this didn't happen.

Instead, he went on to live a life far greater than it might have been had these tragedies never occurred. How was this possible? While one avenue closed, another opened. His hearing was enhanced and combined with his aptitude for music, a devastating fusion was formed.

Soon, he became a musical genius, merging different styles of music and creating songs that captivated millions around the world. Even the apparent limitation of being blind seemed to work in his favour. By reducing the amount of options available to him, he *had* to focus on his music. This combination of application and talent directed him to the top - on a collision course with greatness.

The Hidden Message

So far, every section of this chapter has been subtly shaping your understanding of adversity in an attempt to alter the way you deal with the challenges of escaping The System. The ultimate intention is to move away from The System's understanding of adversity (where it's seen as something that puts an end to your dreams or reinforces your limitations) to one that will facilitate your climb to greatness. This can only occur when you begin to look for *the hidden message* in your adversity.

The next story provides an example of someone who was able to do just that. It focuses on an author, Toni Maguire, who suffered sexual abuse at the hands of her father while growing up. Although her childhood was harrowing, it gave her an insight that brought relief to both herself, and thousands of people around the world, through her subsequent books. This is her story of finding a gift amidst her curse.

When I was growing up, I never told a soul, apart from my mother, about what was happening to me. I didn't dare tell any of my school friends because I was terrified they'd reject me. In those days "nice girls" in Ireland, where I grew up, didn't talk about bad things that happened to them.

The abuse went on between the ages of six and 14 and only stopped when I became pregnant and had an abortion. At that point I told a teacher, who told the police and my father was jailed for three years.

It was only when I moved to England at the age of 18 that I started to tell people what had happened to me. I'd usually blurt it out after I'd had a few drinks, but I never knew quite how to phrase it. I couldn't bring myself to say that my father had raped me for eight years – although that's what he did.

I decided that if I was going to write something, I would have to wait until my parents were dead. Despite all that they'd done – I include my mother in this as she tried to pretend the abuse hadn't happened, even when my abortion was botched and I nearly bled to death – I know the book would have destroyed them.

My mother died in 1998, and my father four years later, I had a sort of breakdown then. I was grieving for the fact that I couldn't miss him because he wasn't a normal father. There was also a sense of emptiness, and writing the book was a way of filling it.

Writing it has given me peace. For years my mother made me feel guilty about the impact my father's imprisonment had had on their lives, but by writing the story down I finally realised that none of it was my fault.

A few of my friends have said that they can't face reading the book – they would rather think of me as the happy person I am today rather than the traumatised child I was then.

Of course, my childhood was horrible, but for the past 30 years I've been happy. I want people who read my book to know that you can come out the other side.[31]

Although extreme in nature, this story provides reassurance if you're struggling through hard times. You have to remember that Toni Maguire dealt with adversity on a grand scale. This wasn't some minor setback or defeat. Her whole life was potentially ruined by the psychological and physical torment she endured at the hands of her father. However, she was still able to take something positive from the experience.

This brave decision speaks volumes about the possibility of *you* finding a gift amidst your curse. It tells you that no adversity, in of itself, has the power to crush your spirit.

Instead, it's about the meaning you attach to that particular event. Therefore, if you *believe in the idea* that your curse is trying to communicate a lesson, or lead you in a new life enriching direction, then it's likely you'll find one.

I've certainly found this to be true. I used to rue the wasted years I spent at university, and in my early 20s, preoccupied with physical ailments like insomnia, IBS, shoulder pain and a bloodshot eye. They took up so much of my mental attention I literally forgot to live and have fun. However, in having to heal myself of these ailments, I gained an in-depth insight into the power of the mind.

These insights served me to great effect while working as a hypnotherapist and then writing this book. I found my gift amidst my curse. If you want to do the same, my advice is to look for what your suffering forces you to learn. If you are unfortunate enough to lose a leg, then perhaps you'll develop an expert insight into leg prosthesis and create one that advances the comfort of millions of amputees. If you're a fringe dweller who doesn't have any friends at school or work, then perhaps you can use this extra free time to throw yourself into an exciting and meaningful dream. If you lose a job you've held for many years, then perhaps you can use the knowledge you've gained to set up in business for yourself. There's a lesson within every curse and when you learn to search for that, instead of getting overwhelmed by the pain, you'll discover a new super power you never previously possessed.

To assist you in doing this, I want you to consider these questions.

- What direction is your adversity steering you in?

- Who are you going to have to become to conquer it?
- What does it want you to learn?

Finally, consider that this is, perhaps, destiny. No matter what you're going through right now, maybe it's the calamity you need to awaken you to your life's mission. As Bob Marley said, *"You never know how strong you are, until being strong is your only choice."* Could your suffering be a sign from The Universe that it's time to break free from The System and live your life's purpose?

The second point of interest from Toni Maguire's story lies in how to *use* the gift you have found. You must to be prepared to *face your demons*. By going into the heart of what has traumatised you, you give yourself the chance to learn. This is exactly what Toni did by writing about her experiences. To relive each moment must have been harrowing but, by doing so, she unlocked the wisdom and insights she'd gained.

Most people would have missed such an opportunity. The System encourages us to deny or disguise personal troubles. We have to maintain this façade that everything's ok and, as a result, barely even admit to ourselves that something is wrong.

Such an attitude will never enable you to use the gift hidden within your curse. While you may not want to tell the world your troubles, you have to be honest with yourself. If your life has lost its sense of adventure, your job leaves you exhausted or your marriage makes you feel trapped; do not let the pretence continue. You may feel scared about being one of the lone voices that doesn't just "get on with things," but by heeding the message that your feelings are attempting to communicate, you'll discover a way out.

Remember, your feelings are there for a reason. In fact, as painful as they may be, they are sacred. Encrypted within their sting is a message. Decode it, and it will lead you through your discontent to your true destiny. Ignore it, and a once in a lifetime opportunity will slip through your fingers.

Embracing Adversity

The cynic might ask whether the rewards of telling her story outweighed the torment that Toni experienced during her childhood. I don't. Adversity is an inevitable part of the human experience. Through lack of knowledge, experience or discipline, you might find yourself in an unpleasant situation. When this occurs, what you have to decide is whether that particular misfortune is going to be the event that signals your defeat, or whether it will lead you to a discovery that will enrich your life.

In Toni's case, she could have refused to tell her story. She would have been within her rights to shut down and claim the sexual abuse she received as a child had permanently ruined her adult life.

This would have been the easier option. By choosing this path, she would've had a legitimate excuse for playing the role of blameless victim. However, as unpleasant as her childhood experiences were, they did give her a unique insight into abuse.

This gift was of great value. By deciding to use it, she

healed the wounds of the past and enriched both her life and the lives of others.

Making this choice is, perhaps, the ultimate indicator of inner strength. For a person to have every legitimate reason to quit, and yet still continue, demonstrates a strength of spirit that can never be contained by The System.

You must remember this the next time you feel that all is lost. As soul destroying as your defeats and failures may be, what makes you great is your ability to always believe you'll emerge triumphant. **And you will.**

The Final Step:
Deciding to be Great

This is the greatest moment of your life and you're off somewhere else missing it!

> - Tyler Durden, *Fight Club*

Hope is a strange quality. While we're taught that it gives us strength in times of need, the other side is seldom explored. Whether it's the hope of promotion, meeting your soul mate, finding your purpose in life or even winning the lottery, the act of hoping for change always carries with it the same connotation. It's a wish that *at some point in the future*, your circumstances, and life, will get better. It's never *now,* and this is the problem.

This difference in time scale makes hope very similar to the pot of gold at the end of the rainbow - the closer you get to it, the further it gets moved away. By hoping, you never grasp what you seek. It always remains the prize you're working towards and that, someday, just maybe, you might claim. Unfortunately, such an acknowledgment of lack, in a reality which is shaped by what you *believe* you already *have,* only sets you up for years of futile longing.

For this reason, you are being instructed *not* to hope for a greater life. Don't spend your days wishing that, at some point in the future, your life will improve. Don't hope that, one day, you'll live the life of your dreams. Don't picture greatness as some far off, barely attainable goal. Instead, know that it happens *now*. See yourself as complete, realise you are good enough and go out and live your life. You don't have to wait; you really can have it now.

While it may take years for the physical completion of your journey, this is no empty statement. From the moment you put this book down; you can live your life with an energy and dynamism that surpasses any material reward. At its core, this is what the quest for greatness is really about. Behind your desire for riches, success and a better life, is the simple need to feel good. **You can do this today**.

Remember, there is no barrier to your happiness apart from the conditions you place on feeling it. Using the strategies in this book you can reframe your suffering, let go of your fears and live in the state of your realised desire. As Tyler Durden says, "*This is the greatest moment of your life*" and if you're hoping for change, bemoaning your fate or struggling to improve your lot, then you're missing out. So, take a deep breath, raise your arms to the sky and realise that *this* is your moment of greatness.

Going Against the Grain

Much of the advice in this book is contrarian. You won't be taught it in school; you won't hear friends discussing it and you'll never read it in a newspaper or magazine. This is because it runs counter to the accepted way of thinking. For example, we're told that hope is humankind's salvation, not a mental block that prevents us from achieving our desires. We're taught to be ever conscious of the need for money, not to follow our dreams and allow our inspiration to act as a guide. We're taught that success is created by working endless hours, playing the game and forcing it to happen; not by letting go of our need to control. And we're taught that failure is final, not an opportunity to learn something new. This knowledge helps us survive in The System. However, what it can't do is show you how to attain something greater.

To do this, you'll have to challenge the accepted way of thinking and accustom your mind to perhaps the most contrarian piece of advice you've read to date - *being great is a decision you make*. It's the beliefs and emotional states you *choose* to have on a moment to moment, day by day basis, that make you great. Very few people are swept along on a tide of greatness. For most, it comes as the result of thousands of small, courageous decisions which, over time, make you unshakeable in your belief and give you laser-like focus. This kind of character is not a pipe dream; it is your birth right waiting to be claimed.

Digesting this final insight may take time. You might find yourself drawn back to The System's understanding of greatness. It's very easy to look upon the achievements of others and revert to type in this way. You think only of greatness with a capital G and those who achieve it are distinctly different or born that way. To think that it's a choice anybody can make seems inaccurate, almost beyond belief.

This is, in part, due to the spotlight phenomenon. Often, we are only made aware of the greats once they have reached their zenith. We see them in all their glory and overlook what can be a long journey (sometimes over 10 years of hard work and commitment). These years are a must for anyone who wishes to excel, but are easily forgotten amidst the magnificence of the end product.

This scrutiny of what it takes to be great must also be applied when considering what it *means* to be great. Do not focus too heavily on the greats we read about in history books or see on TV. By overlooking the thousands, if not millions, of unknown people who have achieved greatness in their particular field, you only add to the confusion surrounding who can, or can't, be great.

This is why the term "personal" greatness is used occasionally in the book. It is included to let you know that ultimately, you are the arbiter of whether you have achieved this level. Your dream is no less valid if you remain unknown. Your purpose in life can still be fulfilled without conforming to The System's notion of greatness.

System Failure

You must understand that greatness will not be put upon you or fall into your lap. You also need to know it's a quality that is accessible to anyone. Even if nothing in your life to date has hinted at the prospect of untapped potential, there is a way of reaching out to something greater than what you've got. All you need is a desire, a goal or something you wish to achieve. You can then put this knowledge to use in achieving that goal and prove to yourself you have the ability to develop and grow. Further goals will follow as you piece together exactly what it is you want to do with your life.

In making this decision, you need to realise you'll be operating outside conventional ways of thinking. If there's one difference between those who are great, and those who struggle to get by, it's found in the way they *think*. Your mind can't stay at The System's level. You must detach your beliefs, attitudes and daily thoughts from the general consensus.

This is the essence of what it really means to escape The System. You may work in it, pay your taxes, own property etc., but you *never* believe in it. That part of you remains untouched. The second you start accepting The System's outlook, the magic will fade. You'll remember that dreams never come true, it's impossible to sustain happiness and that life is full of limitation.

With such a mind-set, it becomes impossible to make the decision to be great. For a start, it's no longer yours to make. You're just an ordinary person who has to put up with an ordinary life. Your future is pretty much set and will stay within the boundaries of normality. In the words of one of my Political Science tutors (spoken when the class was discussing future careers), "*Don't get your hopes up. Nobody really lives an exciting life.*"

Remember, though, you have a choice. The System's reality is not *the* reality. If you choose not to accept it, then a new reality will emerge without the limitations and constraints of the past. There may be a struggle as you battle with old beliefs but, ultimately, The System will bend, not you.

Just look at the examples in this book;

Carl Brashear, once victim of the US Naval establishment's campaign to keep him in what they viewed as his rightful place; eventually honoured with a Public Service Medal from the Secretary of Defence.

Muhammad Ali, vilified for turning his back on America with his refusal of the draft and acceptance of the Nation of Islam; now worshipped as one of history's most beloved sports stars.

Galileo, decried by the religious establishment as a heretic; now declared the father of modern science.

Ironically, it's only by rejecting conventional ways of thinking, and being prepared to challenge the assumptions others take for granted, that you can eventually put yourself in a position where *you* set the agenda.

* * *

A tutor of mine once told me that it's good to end an essay with a quote. He said if someone else has already said it best, and you can't top it, then borrow from them and go out strong.

So, I chose something I think you'll like. Taken from *The Matrix*, it perfectly captures the choice you are now faced with – **Take a leap of faith into the life of your dreams or return to The System's fold**.

Neo offers up the exact same choice at the end of the film. Against the backdrop of luminous green "matrix" digits read the words "System Failure," as he proceeds to narrate:

> I don't know the future. I didn't come here to tell you how this is going to end. I came here to tell you how it's going to begin. I'm going to hang up this phone and then I'm going to show these people what you don't want them to see. I'm going to show them a world without you, a world without rules and controls, without borders and boundaries – a world where anything is possible.
> Where we go from there . . .is a choice I leave to you.[32]

Coaching

Are you serious about escaping The System and creating the life you want? If so, then why not speed up the process by having me coach you? Email me at joe@screwthesystemnow.com to arrange a FREE consultation. This can be done at your convenience and typically takes place via Skype or Zoom.

You can let me know what you're struggling with and I'll explain how I can help. Furthermore, if you quote 'Escape' in the subject bar when you send the email, I'll give you a 25% discount off the first session or package you book.

I can help you;

- Connect with your inspiration, and discover your passion, so you have a clear idea about how to start making a living from something you love.
- Remove limiting beliefs that have been holding you back for years.
- Apply confidence and self-esteem boosting techniques to turn you into a dynamic person capable of living their dreams.
- Free yourself from doubts, fears and negative thinking.
- Stay accountable to the schedule we agree.
- Cope with, and find the hidden meaning, in the adversity you face.

I've been coaching clients in multiple fields for over 15 years. This includes helping tennis players reach national level, removing lifelong bad habits and crippling anxieties for hypnotherapy clients and coaching my readers to find and succeed at the work they love. Email me today at joe@screwthesystemnow.com to arrange your FREE consultation.

Acknowledgments

A great thank to my writing mentor Tom Butler Bowdon. It's no exaggeration to say that *Escape the System* wouldn't be what it is without his input. His wisdom, insights and library of knowledge on all things personal development, helped give the book a direction that became easy to follow. His key advice – break through the surface and bring out your true voice – is something I'd recommend everyone to follow.

Thank to Andy Dalton for his hard work on the website.

Big thanks to my hypnotherapy mentor Tim Martin of the Mind Boutique. Always ready to listen and help, your advice has been key in developing my skills and getting me through the tough times.

To Andy Macro – a VERY big man.

To Claire Daly – Thank you for your undying support and for being a sounding board for so many of my ideas.

To anyone who has reviewed this book, or is going to, thank you so much. It's greatly appreciated.

Endnotes

[1] Suicide is a bigger killer in UK men between the ages of 18 and 34 than AIDS, road accidents and murder combined
https://www.rt.com/news/male-suicide-killer-rate-738/

[2] Prescription drug use in America has risen to over 48% of the population over 12 years old
http://www.cdc.gov/nchs/data/databriefs/db76.htm

[3] Joseph Murphy, *The Power of your Subconscious Mind*, Pocket Books, 2000.

[4] Ross Heaven, *Spirit in the City*, Bantam Books, 2002.

[5] Marianne Williamson, *A Return to Love*, Harper Collins, 1992.

[6] Joseph Murphy with Bill Moyers, *The Power of Myth*, New York: Anchor Books, 1991.

[7] Bruce Wilkinson, *The Prayer of Jabez*, Multnomah Books, 2000.

[8] Bruce Wilkinson, *The Prayer of Jabez*, Multnomah Books, 2000.

[9] Martin Luther King, *The Autobiography of Martin Luther King*, Little, Brown and company, 1999.

[10] Joseph Murphy, *The Amazing Laws of Cosmic Mind Power*, Reward Books, 1965.

[11] *Unforgiveable Blackness*. PBS Home Video. Directed by Ken Burns. 2004.

[12] Wayne Dyer, *You'll See it, When you Believe it*, Arrow Books, 1989.

[13] James Allen, *As a Man Thinketh*, DeVorss and company, 1999.

[14] Trevor Sylvester, *Wordweaving*, Quest Institute, 2003.

[15] T.S. Eliot, *The Hollow Men*, 1925.

[16] Bruno Klopfer, *The Psychological Variables in Human Cancer*, University of California, 1957.

[17] 80% of guests on the Tim Ferriss Podcast have some form of meditational or mind focusing routine http://podcastnotes.org/2015/09/21/the-tim-ferriss-show-5-morning-routines-for-winning-the-day/

[18] Michael Jackson, *Moonwalk,* William Heineman London, 1988.

[19] Joseph Murphy, *The Power of your Subconscious Mind*, Pocket Books, 2000.

[20] Lynn Grabhorn, *Excuse me, Your Life is Waiting*, Mobius, 2005

[21] Malcolm Folley, *Borg vs. McEnroe*, Headline Book Publishing, 2005

[22] Michael Jackson, *Dangerous*, Epic Records, 1991.

[23] Anthony Keidis, *Scar Tissue*, Hyperion, 2004.

[24] Anthony Keidis, *Scar Tissue*, Hyperion, 2004.

[25] *Jerry Maguire*, TriStar Pictures, 1996.

[26] Neil Strauss, *The Game*, Canongate Books, 2005.

[27] Taken from interview with Carl Brashear in special features of *Men of Honour*, 20th Century Fox, 2000.

[28] *Men of Honour*, 20th Century Fox, 2000.

[29] James Allen, *As a Man Thinketh*, DeVorss and company, 1999.

[30] *Pumping Iron*, White Mountain Films, 1977.

[31] Interview from the Real Lives sections of Good Housekeeping circa 2007.

[32] The Matrix, Warner Brothers, 1999.

Printed in Great
Britain
by Amazon

32372003R00176